"Earnie Larsen has an incredible love of the human spirit that reaches beyond the written word and takes hold of your heart. You'll laugh with him and cry with him, but most of all you will be grateful he's in your life. He has honored the reader with *Destination Joy*."
—Claudia Black, Ph.D., author of *It Will Never Happen to Me*

"Earnie Larsen hits a home run once again with his prescription for abundance and joy. As a grateful recovering alcoholic of twenty-two years, I highly recommend Larsen's newest book, *Destination Joy,* to the best people in the world—people in recovery."
—Jim Ramstad, U.S. representative, Minnesota's Third Congressional District

"Thank you, Earnie Larsen, for helping us to see. By 'connecting the dots' of our life experience and going as deep as our pain, we are able to realize that the past no longer has the power to diminish us."
—Joe Anderson, C.A.D.C. III, R.C.S., L.A.D.C., program director, Kinnic Falls Alcohol-Drug Abuse Services, Inc., River Falls, Wisconsin

"Earnie Larsen brings us God's love and encouragement and is drawn like a magnet to the sickest and neediest people in the world. *Destination Joy* will lift many hurting folks."
—Mary Jo Robinson, cofounder, Christ Recovery Center, Union Gospel Mission, St. Paul, Minnesota

"Earnie Larsen has contributed more than anybody I know to the steps needed to reach the sanctuary where joy resides."
—Desmond Kelly, M.D., visiting professor, University College London, and former medical director, The Priory Hospital, Roehampton, London, England

"Congratulations, Earnie Larsen. You have written another phenomenal book, which I am confident will continue to benefit those who are hungering to hear the *music*."
—Nancy Gallagher, I.C.A.D.C., C.G.C., family programs coordinator, Westover Treatment Centre, Ontario, Canada

"If Hazelden's mission is to 'improve the quality of life for individuals, families, and communities,' *Destination Joy* is a blueprint of how to achieve this goal. Larsen maps out a simple, effective way to achieve an enhanced quality of life. Well done!"
—Brian Gallagher, I.C.A.D.C., aftercare coordinator, Westover Treatment Centre, Ontario, Canada

"This is not a book of theories. It will jerk a response from those readers who recognize the lonely place we sometimes reach. It will provide understanding for many who have tried long and hard to move to a better place in recovery but can't open the door."

—Winifred Parry, psychotherapist and director of Addiction Services,
The Priory Hospital, Roehampton, London, England

"If there is anyone qualified in helping just ordinary human beings seek and find a healthier way of life, that person would be Earnie Larsen."

—Adrian B. Capitol, L.A.D.C., day treatment director,
The City, Inc., Minneapolis, Minnesota

"Earnie Larsen has done it again! This book can change your life. Thank you, Earnie, for another contribution to recovering people."

—Linda Gillette, L.A.C., L.S.W., clinical supervisor, Circle of Life
Alcohol and Drug Program, Three Affiliated Tribes,
Fort Berthold, New Town, North Dakota

"*Destination Joy* lets us know that we are lovable, loved, and loving. Larsen helps us to understand that life happens and that with recovery we can and will get through it."

—Carmen Rawe, M.Ed., L.P.C., C.A.D.C. II, consultant

"Knowledge is the greatest weapon for our own Indian people, and for all warriors to reach full strength, they need to read this book, feel the spiritual gift, and reach full recovery from past pain."

—Warren J. Anderson, L.A.C., Turtle Mountain Chippewa Tribe,
Belcourt, North Dakota

"Thank God for Earnie Larsen! *Destination Joy* will set you free. This book is for everyone in recovery and all health professionals. No price can be put on the value of Earnie Larsen's work."

—June Lake, executive director, The Australian Institute
of Counseling in Addictions, Sydney, Australia

"Earnie Larsen has a wonderful insight into the true feelings of pain brought on by the ravages of addiction. Larsen also has a real feel for the joys of recovery. His experience in the recovery field gives him a deep wisdom and understanding of the love and fellowship that comes with recovery."

—Larry Bonniwell, L.A.D.C., director, Christ Recovery Center,
Union Gospel Mission, St. Paul, Minnesota

"Bill W. wrote, 'If more gifts are to be received, our awakening has to go on.' *Destination Joy* provides an excellent road map to follow."

—Donald H. Andrews, associate counselor,
Salvation Army Adult Rehabilitation Center, Akron, Ohio

"Father Joseph Martin once said, 'It's not the degrees or credentials we have but the ability to touch another's heart.' Earnie Larsen has accomplished that."

—Charles DeVries, C.A.S.A.C., substance abuse counselor,
New York State Department of Correctional Services

"The greatest barrier to a joyful recovery is buried in our secrets, wherever and however they were created. Earnie Larsen lovingly shares the road map on how to take the necessary risks to finally confront those last dark secrets that keep many of us from our ultimate goal: being completely happy, joyous, and free. Larsen provides the knowledge and encouragement on trusting the process so we can absolutely enjoy life."

—Boyd Smith, chief operating officer, Cumberland Heights Alcohol
and Drug Treatment Center, Nashville, Tennessee

"Earnie Larsen's *Destination Joy* is an excellent resource; it maps out a plan for individuals in recovery to help them rebuild their lives with joy and abundance."

—Gail G. Milgram, Ed.D., director of education and training,
Center of Alcohol Studies, Rutgers University

Destination Joy

*Moving beyond Fear, Loss, and
Trauma in Recovery*

Earnie Larsen

AUTHOR OF

*Stage II Recovery:
Life beyond Addiction*

Hazelden
Publishing

Hazelden
Center City, Minnesota 55012-0176

1-800-328-0094
1-651-213-4590 (Fax)
www.hazelden.org

©2003 by Hazelden Foundation
All rights reserved. Published 2003
Printed in the United States of America
No portion of this publication may be reproduced in any manner
without the written permission of the publisher

Library of Congress Cataloging-in-Publication Data

Larsen, Earnest.
    Destination joy : moving beyond fear, loss, and trauma in recov-
ery / Earnie Larsen.
        p. cm.
    Includes bibliographical references.
    ISBN 1-59285-037-5 (pbk.)
        1. Recovering alcoholics—Psychology.   2. Recovering addicts—
Psychology.   3. Alcoholics—Rehabilitation—Psychological aspects.
4. Addicts—Rehabilitation—Psychological aspects.   5. Adult child
abuse victims—Rehabilitation—Psychological aspects.   6. Twelve-
step programs—Religious aspects.   I. Title.
    HV5275.L37 2003
    362.29'18—dc21

                                                    2003050819

Editor's note
All references to *Alcoholics Anonymous* are from the fourth edition
(published by AA World Services, Inc., New York, N.Y.).

Cover design by David Spohn
Interior design by Wendy Holdman
Typesetting by Stanton Publication Services, Inc.

Dedication

To those who hear the music.

Recovery and life itself is a kind of music. If you hear the music, the dance makes perfect sense. If you don't hear the music, you never quite understand what all the fuss is about.

Larry hears the music.

I was talking with him before our weekly meeting at the Union Gospel Mission. Ron, an old and dear friend of Larry's, made his uncertain way up the center aisle of the meeting room toward Larry. He obviously had something important to say to his friend.

Larry lit up like a Christmas tree when he saw Ron approach. He always does. Larry understands how difficult it is for Ron to stand out in any crowd, even among his brothers at the Mission. Whatever he had to say, it had to be important for Ron to make this effort to come forward.

Ron had been stomped upon hard by alcoholism, living on the streets and on the reservation before that. He had lost much, but with the help of God and his own innate toughness, Ron had saved the sacred center of his soul. In a week, he was to celebrate his sixth year of sobriety.

Although Ron can't speak in complete sentences anymore, he and Larry communicated well. Larry was making a big deal about his sobriety anniversary the following week. Ron acknowledged Larry's comments; then he pointed his finger several times at Larry. He was asking Larry if he would present him with his medallion. Ron's invitation was better than getting the Nobel Peace Prize for Larry. He told Ron it would be a huge honor to do so. Now it was Ron who lit up like a Christmas tree. The smile of someone who has been truly heard and valued, a need as old as humanity itself, illuminated Ron's scarred, beautiful face.

As Ron turned around and made his way back to the last row where he always sat, Larry turned to me and said, "Didja see it? Didja see it?" Larry had captured the endless mystery of recovery in three words, "Didja see it?" Either you hear the music or you don't. Larry hears the music.

This book is dedicated to all of those in Twelve Step recovery of whatever variety who hear the music.

We feel a man is unthinking when he says that sobriety is enough. He is like the farmer who came up out of his cyclone cellar to find his home ruined. To his wife, he remarked, "Don't see anything the matter here, Ma. Ain't it grand the wind stopped blowin'?"

(Alcoholics Anonymous 82)

Contents

Preface

Dear Friends in Recovery,

Stage II Recovery: Life beyond Addiction was published in 1985, and the sequel, *Stage II Relationships: Love beyond Addiction,* was published two years later. These books explored the rebuilding of life that was saved after breaking the primary addiction. I wrote these books because after many grateful years in the Twelve Step fellowship, I was still experiencing more pain than seemed should fit in the context of a recovering life. The more I talked about what was going on with me, the more people I found who were in the same boat. The books put a name to powerful experiences recovering people felt but had no words to describe—Stage II Recovery. The fact that both are still in publication and the term *Stage II Recovery* is still understood after all this time says they touched a nerve.

Since 1985, I've learned a lot about recovery—both my own and others'. Some of it has been a celebration of gratitude and some a journey through dark, dangerous places I'd just as soon have skipped.

This book was written for you: my brothers and sisters in recovery who are members of this vast Twelve Step fellowship. These pages are for those who have felt the dark and yet hunger for the light. I am writing for and to the countless unsung heroes out there who, on a daily basis, make positive and sometimes heroic decisions that make such a difference in their own and others' lives.

This book is about moving beyond fear, loss, and trauma into joy and abundance. People who survive severely traumatic events often are diagnosed with post-traumatic stress disorder

(PTSD). I am not a medical doctor, so my intention is not to diagnose anyone with PTSD or any other disorder, for that matter. My intent here is to show there are serious and profound implications of childhood abuse in recovery, and until they are dealt with, an increased spiritual life full of abundance and joy simply can't happen.

This book explains the journey to abundance that I and those I am blessed to travel with have been led. As always, take what you like and leave the rest.

Together in gratitude and courage,
Earnie

Acknowledgments

I have a number of people to thank. With special thanks to the Christ Recovery Center of the Union Gospel Mission and the Adult Recovery Center of the Salvation Army and to Corrine Casanova from Hazelden, whose unending encouragement and work made this book better. And with all my heart, I thank and bless all those who cared, stuck by me during the worst times, and told me it would be okay, especially my wife, Paula.

Introduction

For years, many valid but unrelated ideas have been put forth in addiction recovery literature. One example is the emphasis on family of origin material without providing it within the context of a living, breathing model that we can learn from. Unrelated good ideas do not make a model. Only within a model do the ideas come together to form a useable whole. A blizzard of unrelated ideas can be as confusing as they are helpful. For example, consider disassembling a car part by part. Then, lay out the thousand separate pieces on your lawn. They are all perfectly good parts, but until they are put together correctly, all these separate parts do not make a car. You can't drive a thousand separate parts down the highway.

Another way of looking at this is to consider a map cut into many little pieces. The name of a city appears on each piece. The cities are real, they exist, but until you know where they exist in relationship to one another, the map is useless. Without a good, accurate map, it is easy to get lost. This book's goal is to provide you with an accurate map of recovery that allows you to navigate the rough terrain that is part of everyone's recovery journey.

Destination Joy has been carefully organized into three distinct parts. Section 1 lays out the reason and reality behind a recovery model that starts with us first as human beings and then as those afflicted with or affected by addiction. This model shows you how to honor your own story no matter how horrific it is because, ultimately, your truth can only be found in your story. We are our story. Our story is us. Moving beyond sobriety to joy and abundance can only happen in the context of our story. Section 2 reveals the map, or three stages of recovery. The map shows us the path to joy and abundance. Section 3 is about the basics. The map to joy and abundance has always been about the basics. Sometimes we need to be reminded of what those basics are and why they have always been what we need to stay the course.

A Map to Abundance

CHAPTER 1

Learning to Trust Your Story

~

The only truth we will ever find is in our stories. We are our stories. Recovery demands we pay attention to what our stories have to tell us.

Want the best possible insights on recovery? Look at your own life story. Paying attention to your life is the best addiction and recovery education possible. Theory is good, but experience is the only proof. Only low spiritual self-esteem keeps us from seeing the grandeur of our own story. Low spiritual self-esteem is the belief that everyone else's story is full of courage, wonder, and beauty, but not our own. It fails to recognize that God is as active and powerful in our own lives as he is in others. Low spiritual self-esteem blocks us from the truth we need to move forward in our recovery. Truth, of course, comes in different flavors. One type of truth is intellectual and abstract, while another is lived and specific. They each serve an important but different purpose. Intellectual understanding of addictions and recovery is important because nothing is gained by crowning ignorance. We all must find and follow the truth about recovery as it plays out in our own lives, or we will forever be running to others, hoping they can deliver us from the uncertainty we find within. The type of truth that is lived is found in the book *Alcoholics Anonymous,* which Alcoholics Anonymous (AA) members affectionately refer to as the "Big Book." The heart of the Big Book is the personal truth spelled out in the experiences of the stories. Nothing is real until it becomes personal. This is what makes recovery real.

SHARING WITH OTHERS

The Big Book tells us, first of all, to share our experience, not what we know, think, or memorize. Our truth is in our experience. From that comes strength and hope. If we want to know what works, we need to pay attention, to listen, to ask questions of others and ourselves. The answers we find will lead us onward to joy and abundance and light our way forward.

The founders of Alcoholics Anonymous, Bill W. and Dr. Bob, certainly did not sit around some coffee shop or university dreaming up a new theory of treating alcoholism. The Twelve Steps were drawn from the vast, churning, grinding machine of lost souls seeking freedom. It was born in blood, not water. Incredible spiritual power was generated by these two drunks sharing their experience, strength, hope, and wisdom in Henrietta Seiberling's carriage house in 1935. They weren't conjuring up dreams; they were fighting for their lives. In turn, they traded their self-reliance for God-reliance.

They learned the critical lesson of humility by being knocked down so hard neither one knew if he could ever get up. And they wouldn't have gotten up if they hadn't felt the power of fellowship with the God of their understanding and their recovering kin. Bill W. and Dr. Bob felt, saw, touched, and learned from their past experiences. The Twelve Steps are a direct result of those experiences. Bill W. and Dr. Bob learned by doing, and in doing they became the lights in the darkness shining down the corridors of time.

US AND OUR "ISMS"

Without a map, moving forward on our journey of recovery is dangerous and difficult, if not impossible. How could an effective, efficient program of progress be put in place without a map showing us where we are going? The recovery field knows how to arrest addictions. The question is "How do we learn to deal with our lives in a more organized, structured manner after that separation from the addiction—or the devastation caused by a close relationship with an addict?" My personal experience over the years is that there are many who hunger for more in their recovery. We call this rebuilding our lives after arresting the addiction Stage II™ Recovery. In this stage of recovery, we learn how to deal with the pain, shadows, and secrets in our lives. This may seem like a luxury for some people. For many of us, steady progress toward this "more in our recovery" is not a luxury at all. In fact, it may well be the difference between life and death. We all know we either recover or slide down the throat of whatever "ism" is snapping at our heels. Alcohol is the symptom of the disease of alcoholism. Take alcohol out of the equation, and what's left is us—us and our "isms."

From the very beginnings of Twelve Step fellowship, the founders of AA had this ongoing movement in mind when dealing with the "us" that is left after sobriety. On page 132 of the Big Book they admonish, "We absolutely insist on enjoying life."

I fully realize that many in recovery feel no need for ongoing growth aside from going to meetings, doing their readings, and being open to service work. They are doing fine at this point in their recovery, and they want nothing to do with anything like Stage II Recovery. My intention is certainly not to suggest anyone "should" or "needs to" or "must" do anything in the program. What others do in their program is not my business. I have enough trouble working my own program. My intent is to show anyone who is interested one possible road to recovery.

THREE STOPS ALONG THE WAY

This book provides a map, at least one possible map, for those who want and need to take their understanding of recovery and their program deeper. Look closely at these three places along the continuum of your recovery and see if you can relate to any of them:

1. hitting another wall
2. suffering a chronic or periodic relapse
3. hungering for more

1. Hitting Another Wall

This place is about pain. If you had a toothache and went to the dentist, and you were asked which tooth was causing the pain, you wouldn't respond, "I don't know. Pull them all!" What is causing our pain now is the same issue or character defect that caused us pain in the past. It is the same stuff we found the "answer" for in chemicals or in how we acted out "our responsibility" to get a loved one to stop using. It is the same hole in our hearts that the chemicals or failed coping strategies we used in our past promised to fix. As we have said before, alcohol is the symptom of the disease of alcoholism. Take alcohol out of the equation, and all that's left is us. The truth is "I am my problem."

How many times have you heard someone in a meeting say something like, "Booze (or whatever) made me feel confident, strong, brave, smart, good looking, acceptable"? The chemical took us to Oz. But we always woke up in hell. Recovery is learning to deal with life without the crutch. Alcohol and all illegal drugs lie. We all have learned that they promise what they cannot deliver. And yes, we know we have to deal with our character defects. And maybe we thought we dealt with them a long time ago. Yet here they are again. Chances are they are more powerful now than they ever were. A character defect is sneaky—it may lie dormant for a while; then, for reasons we may not understand, the trigger suddenly gets pulled and we light up. Maybe the pain is new. Maybe it was buried so deep we forgot it was there, but like a bone chip working its way up after a calamitous accident, it breaks the surface and feels like it is going to kill us.

We use all the tried-and-true coping techniques that have worked so well for us in the past, but this is something different. In fact, techniques like praying, turning it over, caring, and sharing don't seem to work at this new point in our recovery. The more we work the honesty part of our program, the more all those recovery behaviors scream at us: "What is happening to me? Why now? What is going on with me?" But the abiding question always is, "Am I willing to pay the new price to face whatever is digging its bloody spurs into my tender flesh? If so, then how do I go forward? What do I need to do?" The road leading through this stage of your journey lies in your map of recovery.

All of us in recovery are used to making changes in our lives. Many of the changes are major and take enormous amounts of courage, support, and energy. Recovery is an example of positive change. Since the world is not perfect, and we surely aren't, there is never a time when we can't move further up the hill. Progress, not perfection, has been a saving light for many of us. But how much progress? How much is enough? When is it okay to stop climbing? When is God finished with us?

Hitting this new wall is pretty good proof that God must

not be finished with us. For whatever reason, the pain escalates to a point where "something has to be done" because life once again simply hurts too much. What determines this pain threshold is the amount of pain we are willing to tolerate. We don't have to be around the program long to be amazed at how much pain others are willing to endure. It doesn't matter whether the pain of some unrecognized and unchallenged character defect has come at us with a pounce or a crawl; when it comes, we know we must do something about it. Hitting this new wall is not a step backward in recovery. It is our spirit, soul, and spiritual center asking us to go further. Go within and discover what all the disquiet and anxiety is about. Are you ready to face whatever negative power is running loose and raising hell with what has been a fairly neat, orderly life?

2. Relapse: Chronic or Periodic

Some people are able to carry incredible amounts of pain and not relapse. Others aren't. Relapse is as much a mystery as is the miracle of recovery. Why do some find ongoing recovery without relapse so difficult?

I've learned it is impossible to predict who will "make it" and who won't. Some we would bet are going to fall flat on their faces in a weekend end up getting their one-year, five-year, then ten-year medallions. What is there to do but shake our heads in amazement and marvel at the mystery of it all?

Others who seem not only to talk the talk, but walk the walk, start their recovery like a house afire; then, boom, the tiger eats their soul again. Why? It's not enough to simply say, "They didn't work their program." Of course they didn't. But the question is, "Why didn't they?" On the surface, it looked like they had surrendered and had all the information and intention in the world to stick with their program.

Relapse is always returning to the old way, the old lie, in an attempt to medicate life's pain. Relapse always has the element of unfinished business, lies, and secrets. Relapse is always a matter of failed honesty in dealing with life as it is. Failed honesty creates isolation. It seeks a place to hide until all that's left is our pain and ourselves twisted together like two snakes trying to kill each other. Who wouldn't relapse if they believed that failure and loss were all life had to offer? Mental drunkenness always precedes physical drunkenness.

Every person in recovery has to deal with their version of the "evil committee" in their heads. Some call it "the junkie," "rats in my brain," or "the lie." Whatever the name used, the reality is we all have a magnet drawing us to self-destruction rather than self-compassion, to delusion and denial rather than honesty, to isolation and hiding rather than relationships and honest, loving connections.

Relapse is looking for the right thing at the wrong address. Human beings are made with a hunger for loving connections. Without them, we wither and wobble toward the dark hole that relapse is. Recovery, on the other hand, is learning to love.

No Stranger to Relapse

Audrey was no stranger to relapse. She frequently relapsed early in her recovery from alcohol, pills, and an eating disorder. She said she failed to get into the spirit of recovery even though she practiced it daily. At a recent open meeting, she told how God used her cat, Damian, to develop what she calls "the head to heart feeling." She explained: "My heart was numb my whole life. I couldn't feel anything for anyone including myself. Damian was never a cuddly cat, but one morning he jumped into bed with me and cuddled up next to me like a spoon. I remember that moment distinctly because I was entertaining thoughts of suicide. He continued to have his 'love time' every morning, and slowly I came to know what love felt like and so lost the desire to end my life."

Damian wasn't a thought or a wish to Audrey. He was an experience. His cuddling up to her like a spoon was something that happened. And in that happening was an invaluable lesson. Love trumps isolation. All any of us wants is a bridge off our private Devil's Island. Only love, recovery-love, provides that bridge. Reflect on the story that is your life. Has anything else ever worked for you?

Audrey believes her Higher Power put Damian in her life for that reason. Audrey says, "I think it's too much of a coincidence that this tiny, furry, warm being decided to snuggle me as I was hitting bottom. It was a gift from God." Messages from beyond our understanding can come from anywhere. These messengers or angels are everywhere, trying to break through our walls of fear, delusion, denial, or plain old not paying attention. Damian was just such an "angel" for Audrey.

A number of long-time recovery people who read early drafts of this book said they liked the way all the various stories validated the point I was making. Everybody likes the stories. I explained that I don't use the stories to validate a point; it is from the stories that the "points" come. The stories of recovering people's experiences came first. There are the lessons of what works and what doesn't. There, hiding in plain sight, is what we need to know about recovery. As we develop more confidence in the power and validity of what we have learned along our way, we become less dependent on the needs of others telling us what's what. In each of our stories are all the answers we will ever find, or need.

Personalize It

Have you relapsed? Perhaps more than once? Do you know others in the program who live with an abiding sense of anger, shame, or fear and therefore are in constant danger of relapse? Where does all that pain come from? How do you go about focusing the power of your program on these recovery issues? (A man in one of the groups I go to calls these abiding issues "spiritual sores." It worked for me.)

Look at your story. The answer is there. Think about it. If you relapsed, why? What pulled you back into isolation and fear? What would have helped you do the next right thing rather than the next wrong thing? The willingness to take a stand, to turn around and face what is chasing us, is the necessary task in avoiding relapse. This courageous facing up to our lives as they are, with all the ghosts we may have inherited and created along the way, is the essence of ongoing, lifelong recovery as human beings.

3. Hungering for More

Linda Y. is a hero of mine. She recently celebrated her twentieth sober birthday. She is blessed with an enormous gift of joy. She radiates. She is a perfect example that recovery is a matter of how we live, not just the addictive behavior we stop or arrest. She pays her dues on a daily basis and so reaps the rewards of the promises of AA. There are many (well, not too many) who light up meetings like Linda. Their companionship and presence in the recovering community is a precious gift. Such people have passed beyond focusing solely on slipping backward. What they want is more. More freedom. More peace. More joy. More willingness to carry the message to others who are suffering as they once were.

These blessed people are glorious lights, the first and best fruits of the Twelve Step program, pointing the way for all of us up the mountain of possibilities. In recovery, moving toward abundance is different for everyone. But we all have a distinct still, small, unique voice within coaxing us along what the

Native American community calls the Red Road, which is the spiritual path. We are all called to go higher.

Every spiritual path is about learning to live with more reverence, honesty, and compassion for both self and all those we meet along the way. Spirituality is the realization that since everyone fights a tough battle, it is better to be part of the solution than the problem. Walking that path the best way we are able is a gift. Gifts are mysteries beyond human understanding. We can invite them, but cannot cause them for ourselves, and certainly not for others. We can remove obstacles to spiritual abundance by undertaking serious, honest, ongoing, lifelong recovery. Ongoing recovery is recovery not just *away from* something but, equally important, *to* something. And that something is the safety, gratitude, and reward of a deeper spiritual life.

CAN YOU RELATE?

Do you relate to any of these three "places" on the continuum of your recovery? If so, then this book is for you. If not, then this segment of the journey of recovery, for you, for now, is where you "leave the rest" after you've "taken what you like" from these previous pages.

IF YOU'VE BEEN THERE, YOU KNOW

I encourage you to honor your story no matter how many bad times there may have been. Our story is all we have. It is the raw material we are given to make our existence a thing of beauty. What we have made and can make of those bad times, as bad as they may have been, shall be the most glorious part of all.

We have been there, and we do know. And what we have gained is priceless wisdom earned the only way wisdom is ever earned—by going into fire to get it. We all must leave a gift of blood at the spot where wisdom is won. Isn't that what wisdom has cost you, the price of blood?

If ever a college or university program were created that supposedly conferred wisdom, what would it look like? How would that class be conducted? What would the participants have to do to get their Ph.D.s?

You know. You probably already have a Ph.D. in life.

Everyone in recovery who gets up each morning committed to "practicing these principles in all our affairs" knows. Like you, I know and treasure many people in recovery who may be only semiliterate but who are geniuses in the ways of a life well lived. I seek out these giants so I can stand next to them hoping some small portion of their light may rub off. They are the glory and the treasure of the program. They have learned and in learning have become more than they ever thought possible. And we have learned! Look at your journey. Look where we have been and what has happened and what splendid lessons we have taken away from the fire.

If you've been there, you know:

What it means to be broken. You know the soul-saving lesson of having lost it all so that you may be opened up for more riches than you ever thought possible. We know what it is to hit bottom, to have no idea of where to go or what to do and so are forced to surrender to a Power greater than ourselves. And from that surrender, we are able to lay claim to a Power that truly is without end. How much is that lesson worth?

If you've been there, you know:

The indescribable agony of watching someone you love die an inch at a time from addiction and realizing there is nothing you can do about it. Or worse, thinking there is something you can do about it and that, in fact, you are responsible for the person's sobriety. (Even though half the time you think if the chemicals don't kill him or her, you will.)

But learning, I mean really learning, that we aren't in control of anyone else. None of us are. We love most genuinely by allowing and insisting the other reap the consequences of his or her own behavior. How much is that lesson worth?

If you've been there, you know:

To stop judging others. Our job is not to judge others but to show up with compassion. Our own walk has taught us well enough to seek mercy rather than strict justice. Who are we to cast stones at one another? We learn from the inside out, from having been there, from the responsibility and incomparable honor of being at the other end of the rope when another reaches out for help. How much is that lesson worth?

If you've been there, you know:

God never sleeps and God never leaves. God is even more patient than this disease of alcoholism and addiction. We were never lost because God always knew where we were and was always waiting for that opening to help us get up.

We know what a tap on the shoulder is all about. We know what it means to be found. Many of us can tell you the day, month, year, and sometimes even the hour and minute when we heard that Voice. We know by experience that touch of the divine picking us up. How much is that lesson worth?

If you've been there, you know:

There is no such thing as being hopeless or beyond recall because we were too far gone to be saved. Yet here we are. Imperfect, to be sure. Full of faults and defects and perhaps with a haunted house for a head. But here we are. Upright. Looking forward. Willing to be used in any way our Higher Power wishes to use us in reaching out to others. *Knowing* in our deep-heart that there is no situation that cannot be made better and no human being beyond the reach of grace. How much is that lesson worth?

If you've been there, you know:

As we move through those first agonizing meetings and begin to nibble at the banquet that recovery is, we come to glimpse the possibility that maybe, just maybe, we can win at life. Maybe we don't always have to be the one standing outside in the dark watching others feast on family, fun, and friends. Maybe I, too, can find a way inside. Maybe I, too, can have a seat at the table, and maybe this program is the way. Maybe I can learn that I, too, belong. How much is that lesson worth?

If you've been there, you know:

The greatest treasure life has to offer is not measured in numbers. It is not about material baggage but rather the quality of our friendships. No amount of money can equal the quality of friendships formed in the program. We all know that.

There are those we see or meet in the program whose appearance alone assures us that everything is okay. We are okay. We'll be fine. They, too, have gone through the fire. They know and understand the power of a smile, a nod of recognition, or the subtle squeeze of a hand. They, too, understand the immense power of friendship. And they take the hand of another and then another still. That line of linked hands, souls, and lives goes forward and backward as far as our minds can travel. And God is the glue that holds us all together. How much is that lesson worth?

If you've been there, you know:

We don't have to be perfect to be acceptable. We learn that anyone who demands perfection of us is not to be taken seriously. We are all past imperfect. We learn to love ourselves despite and even because of the crooked timber with which we are made. We come to understand the need to treat ourselves as we treat those whom we love. And when we fail to do so, as we surely will, rather than flog ourselves as in the old days, we learn to pick ourselves up, dust ourselves off, and start over again. We learn to trust that God is in charge and is taking care of us. How much is that lesson worth?

If you've been there, you know:

The promises are for real. Love, peace, self-respect, or family (whether it be an old one or new one) is possible. It is available. It is accessible. We learn that the hardest lesson in recovery is not to give love but to receive it. The greatest gift we give one another is to allow others entrance into our lives. And we learn to stop pushing that love away. For if God is love and God is in people, each time we pushed others away, we also pushed God away. How much is that lesson worth?

UNCOMMON GOODNESS SURROUNDS US

We who have been given the gift of the program are all so blessed. Doesn't your story shout that truth? Surely one of the major blessings is in the people we are given to walk with, our mates in the Twelve Step fellowship. Nowhere in the world could anyone possibly meet a more improbable collection of fascinating characters and clay-footed saints. Central casting in Hollywood could not hold a candle to us.

People do not come into the program because they are healthy. We come in sick. Yet if we hang around, we find an avalanche of uncommon goodness also surrounds us. Jimmy R. had fifty-four years in the program when he died. He went back so far, he used to fish with Dr. Bob. Over the years, he had been an anchor for thousands of new members. Just to be in the same room with Jimmy gave a person confidence and hope. I saw a hundred new members with Jimmy sport the look of little brothers with a trusted big brother. The look said something like, "I'm here with him. We're friends. So, I am somebody too."

The last dozen years of Jimmy's life were a constant struggle with chronic pain because of a nerve disorder. So bad was the pain that Jimmy had to all but quit his beloved Friday night meetings. Still, his buddy Duane called him every week to see if he was up to going. One bitter cold Friday evening in

January, Duane hobbled with emphysema, pulling his oxygen tank behind him, when he came to get his friend, Jimmy. When, as Vince Lombardi said, fatigue would make cowards of us all, I think of these two old men. I picture them some twenty years ago on that cold, cold evening: Jimmy so tall and frail that a breeze would blow him over, and Duane huffing and puffing in the –30°F weather. But there they were, going to their meeting. And here I am, many years after the death of both of these giants, still basking in their glow and telling you about them. I once asked Jimmy why he went to such effort to get to a meeting when he surely was beyond getting thirsty. He just smiled and said, "I don't go for me. Maybe there is someone I can help at the meeting." Then he threw in his favorite program saying: "You know, program isn't a gift. It is a debt." There is uncommon goodness.

This book has been written for the long line of millions whose linked hands and hearts stretch all the way back to a sitting room in Akron, Ohio, in 1935. Here, God let go a mighty wind that would circle the globe. It was a wind not carried by the mighty and powerful, as those in the program know so well, but by those in the rank and file who are given the responsibility to carry the message.

These pages are for those who understand that for this wind to be made available for those who seek it—we are responsible.

QUESTIONS

1. What does the phrase "low spiritual self-esteem" mean to you?
2. How has the meaning of that phrase affected the quality of your recovery?
3. What are three of the greatest lessons you have learned upon reflecting on your unique life story?

MOVING ON TO CHAPTER 2

A map of recovery is essential in order to answer the following questions: Where are we going? What is our direction? How shall we know if we are moving straight and true or not?

A Map to Abundance:
A Spiritual/Human Model of Recovery

We are human beings before we are either the afflicted or the affected. We recover first as humans. Our deepest needs as human beings are the spiritual needs of being loved and accepted. How those needs are met in our earliest years affects us the rest of our lives. Some are luckier than others in having these needs met.

WHY A MAP OF RECOVERY? WHO NEEDS IT?

Who needs a map of recovery? We all do. Maps give us direction so we don't get lost. Maps can also show what to expect along the way. If we know what is approaching, a rough road doesn't throw us into discouraging fits of frustration and confusion.

Have you ever felt lost or stuck in your recovery because your map just didn't go as far or show you as much as you needed it to? I have. At times, my too-limited map of recovery didn't show me enough, so I hit the wall so hard my teeth rattled. I didn't know why I hit those walls. They made me feel crazy. They made me want to do anything to avoid the confusing yet terrifying work facing me. A map that clearly showed where I was and what I could expect would have made passing through these dark, dangerous places a great deal easier.

AN INVITATION TO GO DEEPER

For years at a time, a person's recovery may go just fine. No hidden obstacles or detours are apparent. We understand what we need to do and why. Going to meetings, working with a sponsor, daily reading, being of service, making regular conscious contact with our Higher Power lead automatically to a higher road. Recovery is working. Then, suddenly, or for others more gradually, this march forward grinds to a halt. Shadows of doubt and discouragement arise from somewhere. Our steadily increasing spirituality seems to decline. As grateful as we are for the incredible gifts recovery has given us, we now obviously need something new. Actions we took in the past no longer seem to get the job done—or at least not in the same way.

If someone is ambushed in recovery by these feelings of lost momentum and doesn't know what is going on, it is natural to think, "I'm right back where I started. All the work of these past years in recovery is wasted. I guess I'll never get it right." It's a short step down from there to depression, discouragement, and defeat. If this state of discouragement is not reversed, relapse follows in one form or another. A comprehensive recovery map shows that this point of intense discomfort is on the map—it is just life doing what it always tries to do, which is to take us deeper. The business of life is life itself. Hitting such a wall is not the result of failed effort but rather an invitation to go to a deeper level of spirituality. A good map clearly shows that all the good work we have done up to this point is not wasted at all. In fact, it was necessary to bring us to this point of growth, no matter how unsettling or difficult it feels. At this point of hitting a new wall, we often say with real frustration, "This stuff again? I thought I dealt with all that a long time ago." We probably did. We dealt with it as we were able to at the time. But now we are able to deal with it on the deeper level that this new/old pain is coming from. The discomfort, then, is not a failure but an opportunity to work a deeper and better program.

People active in recovery know there's no such thing as co-incidence. We know there are angels at the door, leading us on even if we don't recognize them as such at the time. What we see as a frustrating blockage may be a clear voice calling, "You've done great so far! Now, let us take another step."

This attitude of choosing to be honest, open, and willing to the spirit of the program, which is all about change and growth, is painted in sharp detail by the following story:

> In the 1960s, there was a Vietnam War protest in front of the White House on a cold, rainy day. As long as the TV cameras were rolling, the large crowd marched, chanted, and even tried to carry lighted candles in the wet wind. When the cameras left, so did the crowd, except for one man. He remained standing on the corner with his soggy sign and drenched candle. A fellow pro-tester hurrying by said, "Come on. The protest is over. Let's get out of the rain. Besides, you don't think one man can change them, do you?" The lone warrior said, "I'm not here to change them. I am here so they don't change me."

This man knew who he was. He knew what he was about and acted from an inner conviction. This same attitude defines those of us who work our program: The point is not just to be-long or to have a place to go, but to have an inner commitment to follow, in a searching and fearless manner, where the Voice that brought us to the program in the first place now urges us to go.

GOING DEEPER: ESSENTIAL PRINCIPLES

Our Voice always urges us to go deeper into life. Understanding the call to go deeper into life flows from these two principles:

1. In recovery, we are first of all human beings.
2. All human beings have a hunger for love and belonging at their core.

I have observed these principles and how they get acted out in practice countless times by people I consider heroes and giants in the field, and whom I am proud beyond words to call my friends.

Principle 1: We Are First of All Human Beings

We start our map of recovery, then, from the standpoint that people in recovery are first of all human beings. We are more than our disease. It matters where a person starts his or her understanding of recovery. There is a difference between starting from the understanding that we are first of all human beings as opposed to starting from a label such as *addict, codependent,* or *shame-based.*

There is a difference between dealing with "recovery from addictions" as opposed to dealing with "recovery as a human being." The statement "I am first of all an addict" defines the person as a disease. The disease then defines the limit of a person's recovery.

Are we addicts who happen to be human beings or human beings who happen to be addicts? How a person answers that question matters. Take, for example, Andy, a professional electrician who was nearly ten years sober before he recognized his inability to be part of a loving relationship. Needless to say, his wife came to this realization long ago. At first Andy held on to his old but now fading understanding of recovery as sobriety like a drowning man grabbing onto a life raft. His attitude shouted, "I am sober! What the hell else does she want?"

But Andy was a good man, and a brave one. He believed in the honest, open, and willing aspects of the program, even if he desperately didn't want to be any of the three. Slowly he opened up to a wider, deeper, more spiritual understanding of his recovery. He put it this way: "If I keep changing light-bulbs when what is wrong is a short in the cable running to the house, I'll never get the lights to stay on. Burned-out bulbs need to be replaced, but it doesn't help much if it's the cable that is broken. Sooner or later I have to dig up the cable and fix it." I wanted to give him the Medal of Honor for his bravery.

A sober addict is a long way from being a healthy human being. Yet while addiction and recovery are best understood in a spiritual light, there still are physical elements to addiction. Take, for example, alcoholism. If the problem were strictly a physical issue, then when the chemical was removed from the alcoholic, the problems would end. But we all know that isn't the case. This is precisely because of the spiritual aspect of ad-diction. There is no time an addict can ever safely return to the use of mood-altering chemicals. There are stacks of corpses eight miles high out behind the barn that prove, for an alco-holic, that one drink is too many and a thousand is not enough.

Chemicals Medicate Pain

A wise counselor I knew at a hospital-based treatment center lectured around the statement "chemicals medicate pain." His point was that the first step in recovery must focus on the chemical. Nothing good is possible for an addict until sobriety is won. But at some point, if a person's program does not focus on the pain in his or her life, then of course the person will return to the chemical, sooner or later. A uniquely clear picture of recovery emerges when an addict is seen first not as an addict or someone terribly damaged by living with an addict, but as a human being. We are first of all human beings. We recover as people, not just as chemical dependents, gambling addicts, food addicts, sex addicts, or those in close relationships with them.

This counselor would then drive his point home by saying: "Our chemical dependency unit is on the fourth floor of this hospital. The fifth floor is the cancer unit. Let's say there is some poor man up there suffering terribly from bone cancer, and he is given morphine for his pain. Take the morphine away, and what does he have? Take your alcohol away, and what do you have?" His example made it quite clear that, at some point, the recovering person must learn to deal with the pain in his or her life. After all, this pain was there before the alcohol. In fact, this pain has increased during the years of use. You can bet that the pain will return with a vengeance after sobriety is won, which means when the medication has worn off.

If winning the war of abstinence from alcohol is the only real goal of recovery, then what happens after abstinence? What do we do now that recovery has won? Recovery then is like being at a dance when, all of a sudden, the music stops. How can you dance when there is no music? Just recently I heard a radio ad for a cancer hospital that contained this same idea. Their catch line was, "We don't treat cancer. We treat patients." We are more than our disease!

Abstinence is a huge aspect of an addict's life, but it's not the only one or the last one. A longtime sober and well-recovering alcoholic at the countdown of sobriety at the 2000 International Convention of AA in Minneapolis, Minnesota, said to me, "You know, countdowns are fun, but recovery isn't about length of time. It is about quality of life." How right he was.

Principle 2: Every Human Being Hungers for Love and Belonging

The basic truth here is that every human being is born with a hunger for love and belonging. This is the "good stuff" we spend our lives either enjoying or pursuing. Very little of our lives are black and white. We live life in various shades of gray. But there are certainly those who enjoy easier access to this good stuff than others. Being able to get to this good stuff makes a difference in the quality of our lives and, therefore, our recovery since our lives *are* our recovery.

From a spiritual/human standpoint, no matter how far we sail away from home or how badly damaged our spirits become, we are always trying to satisfy our souls. Our deepest hunger is always about those deep connections that most make us human. No matter how twisted the attempt or tragic the behavior, we are all trying the best we can to get down the road that leads to the home we may never have had. Addictions are a substitute for the real thing. Recovery is finding and moving deeper into that real thing. An old AA saying, "Every alcoholic hopes to find God at the bottom of the bottle," says it about as well as words can tell the story.

When access to love, acceptance, and belonging is denied, especially in childhood when our foundation is formed, something tragic happens. The process that always begins with this denial of love and acceptance, our deepest needs, has many names, such as the "ism" of alcoholism, codependency, shame-based, adult child, and emotional and spiritual immaturity. When the question is about human well-being, all there ever is at the core of the matter is love and the damage caused by love denied, especially when that denial (and betrayal) happens in childhood. Recovery, from a spiritual standpoint, is climbing back over the carnage done by consistent, often violent, love denied. This love is first denied by others; then we deny it to ourselves. We do not do this because we are stupid, evil, and deserving of the negative consequences of this process. We do it mostly because we don't know any better. Our maps aren't good enough. We don't recognize the difference between being and acting out who we were told we were "back then," and who we can be and how we can act now, once we take back the power to decide. But if we don't see the difference between "then" and "now," we don't have a choice.

I do not mean to sidestep the question of evil and free will. There are those, the founders of AA tell us, who will never achieve sobriety. They are the "unfortunate ones" constitu-tionally incapable of honesty. There are those among us also who, for whatever complex reasons, have seemingly been to-tally, helplessly captured and destroyed by the cruel selfishness they were taught and then practiced. They rode the back of the tiger and were finally eaten by it. There are those among us be-yond recall.

But who among us really knows which ones are "hopeless" and which ones aren't? There are scores of people who everyone thought were hopeless cases. Then, something happened. A light. A miracle. We were called to a different life. And in every case, the miraculous emergence from the cocoon of spiritual slavery wasn't initiated by whips and clubs, though often enough it occurred when we became unwilling to bear any more pain. This first breakthrough into life is always a movement to-ward truth and honesty. No matter how far down we go or how far gone we are, a first step is always a movement away from ad-dictive living and toward integrity and self-respect.

ALL OTHER GODS SPEAK OF THIS GOD

If the first step in designing a map of recovery is stating the basic principle that we recover as people first and foremost, that means we are all born—addict and nonaddict alike—with an endless hunger for love and community. By stating this premise, we have laid the foundation for a spiritual/human understanding of recovery. Whatever else addictions are about, they all are rooted in soul hunger—the domain of spirituality. My experience is that all roads around, about, and in recovery lead to this fact. As far as recovery is concerned, it is all spiritual. And spirituality is always about love. And love is always about healthy connections.

Holding this view of the centrality of spirituality in recovery puts us in some pretty elite company. Bill W., the cofounder of Alcoholics Anonymous, died in 1971. Lois, his wife, lived until 1988. After Bill's death, Lois carried on as the emotional center of the Twelve Step movement. Lois was asked, after Bill died, if she thought of the spiritual side of the program. She said, "There is no spiritual side. It is all spiritual."

In like manner, Dr. Bob, the other cofounder of the Twelve Step movement, was the spiritual pillar during the program's rocky beginning. Beloved Dr. Bob passed away in 1950. An associate of mine was at a talk recently given by Dr. Bob's son, Smitty. He recounted Dr. Bob's last words to Bill from his deathbed: "Prince William," Bob said, "we have a good thing going here, don't louse it up." Bob was telling Bill to keep ego and pride out of the recipe lest he ruin what they were all about. A bloated or deflated ego always blocks spirit. It has been said that the alcoholic is an unfortunate combination of an egomaniac sitting on top of monumental insecurity.

The Twelve Step program was founded to be a method of spiritual living. The program was and is all about finding and practicing spirituality no matter how far we think we may have turned our back on all things spiritual. Spirituality is all about finding our way home. Recovery is about achieving whatever degree of abundant living we can by living "these principles in all our affairs."

But we do not have to rely on Bill W. and Dr. Bob or go back to our beginnings to see the truth of recovery as spiritual. All we have to do is look at our own experience of recovery and all the other miracles of recovery surrounding us.

What is your recovery story? Who made a difference to you early on (or later) in your recovery? Recovery stories come in endless variety and beauty, yet the core is always the same—the heart was touched. The spirit was found. A long bolted and rusted door that kept us forever in exile finally creaked open. For some, the door was blown open in a white-light experience. For others, the opening was gradual and quiet. However it happened, the experience pointed us in a direction we thought we never would or could travel.

RECOVERY IS ALWAYS ABOUT LOVE

While conducting recovery seminars and conferences, I always stress that from a spiritual/human perspective, recovery is always about love. But words like *recovery* and *love* are just that, words. It is the experience that provides the power. I ask the conference attendees to reflect, look within, and tell me a story about their own or someone else's recovery. Initially, this "love stuff" sounds so vanilla until we tell our stories. Then it becomes clear that recovery-love experienced in the flesh, in the here and now, is the heart and soul of recovery. Recovery always has been and always will be a love story. Have you not found it so?

"I DON'T KNOW WHAT LOVE IS"

Countless people have no idea what love is. These unfortunate people never saw it, never felt it, and were never schooled by it. For them, entering the realm of recovery-love is like backing, blindfolded, onto a street of crazy drivers. For these people, the learning curve of recovery-love runs straight up.

At a recent recovery conference, my presentation, as it always does, focused on recovery-love as the only way I've ever seen recovery work. I spoke of the damages done by our inner dragons and monsters, which once seemed invincible, being healed with love found. After the conference, Robert, a tough-looking young man with prison tats on his arm and steel in his eyes, approached me. Despite his defiant appearance, I could see there was someone else living behind his attitude and posturing. There also was someone in there saying, "Don't be fooled or scared off by my mask. I'm lost in here, but I am worth coming to find. Find me. Please, don't walk away."

The first words out of Robert's mouth were: "I don't know what love is. I don't know what the hell you are talking about. I think you lie. People just aren't like that. I don't believe you." Keep in mind that he sat at the conference all day listening to ideas he "didn't believe." He could have left at any time, but he chose not to. The recovery-love stories I was talking about (it's all just theory until it gets acted out in our stories) somehow spoke to a place he had long ago deserted.

He gave me his address, both mailing and e-mail. (His e-mail began "IDGAF": "I don't give a f——") But there he stood, his small but persistent inner voice calling out. He responded to that voice by attending the conference, approaching me, and reaching out to me, taking the huge risk that I might leave him in the dust as everyone else in his life had. Behind all the anger and pose, he was scared to death, but the music was reaching out to him.

Millions of people just like Robert have no idea what love is. This is because they were broken like twigs from their earliest days. Physical predisposition and the wild rush to escape this terrible pain of love denied drove them into the arms of chemical relief. When I got home from the conference, I contacted some peers who know all about prison tats and steely eyes. They carry the message of hope, courage, and love with fine passion and enthusiasm. They are what the music is all about. It is hard to dismiss someone who has been there. I set a few of these God's dogs loose on Robert. They will follow up and track him down. They will back him into a corner where there is no possibility of hanging on to his ruined shield of "no one cares" and "IDGAF." They will meet his bleeding soul face-to-face, and Robert will learn there is nowhere to hide, not from these Twelve Step warriors and the God who is the leader of the pack.

RECOVERY IS NOT PERFECTION

We in recovery are not perfect. Often we fail miserably. Yet at our best, what we offer each other and anyone who seeks it is access to the really "good stuff." Access to recovery-love that, at its best, melts petrified tears and provides a home where there was none before. Recovery-love is powerful. It lights up the sanctuary of the soul of recovery.

Recovery-love, of course, is different from love in the way our society usually means it. Unfortunately, the media defines *love* as "what's in it for me?" "I'll hang around as long as it's convenient," or "it is a word I use to con someone else and get what I want." No wonder we live in such a violent, addicted society. We no longer even have a word that names the hunger in our souls. Hunger, especially spiritual hunger, without remedy always leads to sick, sad, violent people. The inner chaos made of our unanswered spiritual yearnings is the womb of addictions.

Recovery-love is music for those who can hear. It makes royalty of us all.

If you made a list of the marvels you have seen in recovery, what would be on your list? What miracles have you witnessed? What royalty of the spirit have you seen parade through your life? And when you make your list, look at it again. Are you looking at anything but the bright face of love in one form or another? Is there anything else? What else has made a difference to you in your journey of recovery?

QUESTIONS

1. What is the difference between understanding recovery as first being an addict as opposed to first being a human being?
2. What are the two deepest spiritual needs of all human beings? What does that have to do with your recovery?
3. What has helped you the most in your recovery?

MOVING ON TO CHAPTER 3

If recovery is a human journey and not just separation from addictions, what ground does the map cover? What is the topography we must negotiate on our way to joy and abundance? What is the process traveled in a spiritual/human model of recovery?

The Stages of Recovery: Going as Deep as the Hurt

Everyone gets hurt in life, but not everyone gets hurt to the same degree. The depth of the damage becomes the depth of the spiritual blockage we experience in recovery. Recovery must go as deep as the blockage the damage has caused.

Recovery is the gradual, step-by-step process of going to whatever level the damage exists. In this context, viewing recovery as happening in several stages is helpful, if not essential. Each stage or level is different and requires its own set of tools. By entering a deeper level of recovery, a new understanding is necessary. It's not about "outgrowing" the Twelve Steps. I do not believe that can be done. But the challenge to be "searching and fearless" doesn't end with sobriety or our first Fourth and Fifth Steps.

A long-cherished program slogan is "You can exhaust yourself, but you can never exhaust the program." I totally agree. Yet fidelity to the program also means we may well have to extend ourselves and go where we would rather not (and often dig our heels in all the way to China) to reach the deeper riches of the program. The concept of being honest, open, and willing also does not stop with sobriety.

In the first draft of this book, I devoted a dozen pages to committed, hardworking people in the fellowship who regularly attended meetings yet, strangely, never talked about the real pain in their lives. They eagerly talked about their addictions, but not about their lives. I've met these people everywhere along the recovery road, just as you have. Considerations of space would not permit their stories to be told here. But any of you who have been in the program a while may be able to relate to this strange situation where we go to group but do not talk about the pain caused by the character defects we identified in Step Four and (we hope) shared in our Step Five. Haven't you more than once ground your teeth at the pain still in your life and wondered why? Why is it still with me? Why does it seem to get worse with my increased awareness? This book was written in the fondest hope that it will provide both insight and direction that will enable you to go further down the road in your recovery to joy and abundance.

DIVIDING RECOVERY INTO STAGES

The three stages of recovery are Stage I, Stage II, and Stage III. Dividing recovery into three stages seems to make sense. These stages relate to the depth to which we have been damaged along the way, both by others and by ourselves. This damage then blocks the spiritual growth that allows us access to the connections our lives so yearn for. Each level of hurt demands to be dealt with. But the same tools don't work equally well on each level. Knowing what tools the job requires is not only helpful, it is often critical. I recall a friend of mine in grade school trying to measure a length of board he was going to saw using his suspenders as a yardstick. He couldn't figure out why his mark on the board kept changing on him. Suspenders are fine tools, but they don't work very well as a yardstick.

Let's look at these three stages of recovery. As you consider them, ask yourself, "Can I relate to this? Do these stages appear in my story?"

STAGE I, II, AND III RECOVERY

Stage I Recovery

Stage I Recovery is arresting the addiction or dealing with a crisis. This stage requires that all our energy and attention be focused on the issue at hand. If we have an arrow hanging out of our back, no one cares at the moment who shot the arrow or how it got there. First things first. The arrow hurts, so the first order of business is getting the arrow out and stopping the bleeding.

For all the mystery that might exist around an addiction, the recovery field knows pretty well what it takes and how to arrest that addiction. We know how to do intervention, assessment, and treatment. We know how to do crisis management. We have methodologies that work, which include Twelve Step programs. We know how to get people standing up and facing forward if they are ready.

Stage II Recovery

Stage II Recovery is about doing life management work. The focus of Stage II is not the addiction itself, but the habits and patterns at work beneath the addictions. Stage I Recovery is about stopping. Stage II Recovery is about asking why. It is about understanding the triggers and the imprinting that left us vulnerable in the face of so many powerful substitutes for the "real stuff."

Stage II is about seeking out the tools and support to take adult responsibility for our lives. It's about gaining separation from those old patterns and, slowly but surely, with support both human and divine, choosing a new healthy road. Stage II Recovery requires discipline, practice, and the ability to refuse to let the past rob us of our present. Choosing this new, healthy road isn't as easy as it sounds. The assumption is that we know and recognize the difference between the past and the present as we go about our daily business. Often this is not the case at all. And if we don't recognize the difference between an impulse from the past and our current situation, how are we supposed to make free choices about how we respond to those situations today? Without this recognition and the decisions it calls for, we never do have a present. All we have is an endless recycle of the past.

Stage II Recovery answers will seldom be found in Stage I Recovery groups. They have different focuses, and that's okay. Stage II tools will not be adequate for a Stage I toolbox. The focus and purpose is not the same as Stage I. Keep in mind, one stage is not better than another. There can be no Stage II if Stage I has not been won. First things first. Sobriety is always first. But recovery does not end with sobriety.

Our Higher Power calls us to even deeper levels of growth and recovery. And that deeper level, whatever it may be, can only be gained by a willingness to go as deep as the damage that keeps us from our spiritual destiny of joy and abundance that was ours at the moment of our birth.

Stage III Recovery

Survivors of childhood abuse do not lead the same kind of lives as those spared abuse in their formative years. Their brains have not developed the same. They organize information and sensations in their brains differently. They hear and see different things when they close their eyes.

I am not a medical doctor. I make no diagnosis about abuse or its medical designation as post-traumatic stress disorder. My only intent is to make others aware that there are serious and profound implications of early trauma and abuse for those people seeking recovery and an increased spiritual life. That is what we deal with in Stage III Recovery.

The effects of abuse, of course, are not "one size fits all." Even though there is a psychological designation with established criteria and diagnosis for the damage caused by abuse, we express it in different ways. Every abuse survivor is not affected to the same degree or hurt in the same way. There are too many variables.

But if there is early, intense, consistent abuse in a person's life, the damage of that abuse must be understood and faced before he or she can move on to the joy and abundance spelled out in the promises stated in the Big Book.

WHERE THE ROAD GOES

All Stage II and Stage III Recovery issues are about bringing forward early, negative imprinting into our present consciousness. Before we do that, we must come to understand what this negative force or evil tide is and how it affects us. This "lie" we have unconsciously built our lives around from the beginning must be dealt with. When this negative process has control of our lives, we respond to present situations as if we were still living in the early situations over which we had no control or choice.

We are meant to have genuine choices as adults. To realize those choices, we must learn to mentally and emotionally separate from that powerless, helpless child of the past. We must then learn to make decisions in the here and now based on who we choose to be as adults. Recovery beyond sobriety is learning to be an adult, not a terrified, angry child forever acting and reacting to yesterday in an adult body.

Many coming into the program negotiate Stage I Recovery. Through the true and astounding experience of their First Step, they achieve sufficient separation from their active addiction to make a truly free choice. The miracle begins to unfold as they begin. They are embraced into a recovering community, learn to attend meetings, become increasingly willing to take in the wisdom of the program, read the Big Book, acquire a sponsor, court God as a friend, and set sail on their journey to joy and abundance.

As they continue on this track, the honeymoon often fades. Sooner or later, a head-butting and heart-bruising encounter with another level of recovery occurs. Old living problems come on with renewed strength. By failing to understand that there are stages of recovery we must go through, we can easily become discouraged. We ask: "Why isn't the old, warm recovery feeling still there? What am I doing wrong? After all this time, why does life still get so confusing and messy? Why is there still such a pull to the dark side? When does recovery ever get just plain easy?"

Questions like these are sure signs that it is time for Stage II Recovery. A new level beckons, requiring its own First Step and its own methodology. Sobriety may have been learned; now the task is to learn to live.

As people get Stage II help and learn to negotiate their inner landscape, new joy flourishes. With Stage II Recovery comes a renewed sense of power to manage life. Separation from the old lies is gained. Old triggers no longer have the same power to control our lives. New patterns begin to develop slowly and become realistic alternatives to the old self-destructive patterns. We begin to live by our new truth rather than our old lie. For many, this Stage II Recovery road takes us home. Life still has its peaks and valleys, but we know what we're dealing with. Whether we turn that information into wisdom by practicing our new truth is up to us. Just as AA will ruin a recovering person's drinking forever, a person's Stage II understanding will ruin forever excuses like "I don't know why I keep doing these things" or "I'm so confused, no wonder I relapse all the time."

We may come to this doorway leading to Stage II Recovery and decide, that's it. No more. We have dealt with all the hurt and pain we are going to. We may feel the tug to go further and sense there is something out there or down there inside of ourselves, hiding, and it scares us to death. Whatever "it" is, its power is so strong it turns our spiritual and often our physical legs to jelly. It makes us quake with fear. It fills our heads with howls. We may say to ourselves: "I have come far enough. I don't care about being better. The price is too high. I just don't care. I can't climb any higher."

It is not our job to judge one another. If where we are is as far as we can go, then that is as far as we can go. In fact, others may be many miles farther up the hill than we are. Who knows anything about another's hill, anyway?

There are others who have a concealing smile and eyes as dead as smoked glass. When they recount stories of profound abuse, they shock even those who have seen and heard it all. But to them, it's all just "normal." Everything about them shouts, "I simply don't care." Like our friend Robert in chapter 2, despite this attitude, they show up at conferences or meetings, if only to tell us how much they don't believe in recovery. But their presence speaks louder than their words. People with vision and their ears attuned to the music of the human drama hear differently. They hear, beneath the hurt, a cry of someone lost, begging us not to leave, to see beyond the smoke and find that lost person worthy of fighting for.

They are being chased down the long, dark corridors of life. At first, what is chasing them feels like a dog from hell bent on tearing them to pieces. But after a while, if they find the right tools and the right people to accompany them, they realize that they are being chased by something far different from an apparition from hell. They are being chased by the light. And in that light, we come to understand that our demons are but our angels gone astray. Our demons are the "wrong address" where we sought our angels all along. But now we see, at least better. Now we know the direction we are headed, the direction made real by our oh-so-very-real deci-sions. And the rewards we collect along the way are called joy and abundance.

ANGER AS POWER

Anger is always an issue in recovery. Anger is the emotional re-sponse to perceived injustice. The deeper the damage, the deeper the injustice, and therefore the deeper the anger. Anger is an emotional fire capable of giving both life and death. Most of us know all about the negative aspects of anger, but what about the positive side?

What about using our anger as a kind of emotional light-ning bolt that motivates us to stand up to the wrongs of the past? What about using anger as an ally to give us the strength and determination to say: "Here it stops. No matter what I have to face and what I have to do, by God, I'll do it. Recovery isn't just about me. It is also about those who come after me and who will take their lead from me. However bitter the water that came down to me, from me onward it will be different. It will be better"?

Anger is power, and we have a choice regarding what we will do with it. Our suffering must have meaning, or we suffer for nothing. Meaningless pain is intolerable. Pain is turned to power if we will only hold it up to the light of recovery. What a fine cosmic joke it is to take the source of so much of our trou-bles and turn it around to be used as an equally powerful mo-tivation to build rather than destroy. Whatever happened in the past can't be changed, but you can build a cathedral in the present over the ruins of the past.

We can use many reasons to block ongoing recovery. The questions ultimately become: Is it worth it to take another step forward? Are we willing to try? Are we willing to surrender that last locked door? And if we are, will anyone else go with us?

NO ONE GOES ALONE

Who we are says nothing about who God is, but it says everything about who God is to us. Recovery is the process of finding both self and God. Some would even say self *in* God. We cannot successfully seek God without seeking or finding self. We cannot successfully be intimate with God without learning to be intimate with ourselves.

God fuels recovery. Recovery changes us from the inside out. Recovery is not a coat to be put over ourselves to disguise what's underneath. For example, a fearful person who puts on a recovery coat but fails to conquer his or her fear is still ridden bareback and spurred hard by that fear. A person who tries to establish intimate connections with others, including God, by substituting control, domination, passivity, or giving things rather than self is still left with only a substitution for the real thing.

There is no going to God or recovery without also going to self. Only surrender to God brings forth recovery from those shadowy, hidden depths. To avoid or ignore these hidden depths is to deny the intent and passion of the miracle begun in 1935 with Dr. Bob and Bill W. When they heard the call, they got up and followed, wherever the path led.

QUESTIONS

1. Explain the meaning of Stage I as it relates to your lifelong recovery.
2. Explain the meaning of Stage II as it relates to your lifelong recovery.
3. Explain the meaning of Stage III as it relates to your lifelong recovery.
4. Explain the meaning of joy and abundance as it relates to your lifelong recovery.

MOVING ON TO CHAPTER 4

And so recovery, as both arresting addiction and taking wing after that, is all about spirit and spirituality. What is there to be said, if but a little, of this bottomless well of living water we call spirituality?

CHAPTER 4

Spirituality: The Voice of God

~

We are not human beings trying to be spiritual. We are spiritual beings trying to be human. Recovery is our effort to live the spiritual life we were made for.

Any book on recovery, however it is approached, would be incomplete without clearly stating that there is no recovery without spirituality. Simply stated, recovery is spiritual growth. Those of us in recovery have met the God of our understanding. Who has better experienced "if God is love then love is God" than us in Twelve Step fellowship?

GOD REACHES OUT TO US

Recently, a brother in the fellowship called me from Canada. He was having a tough time dealing with family illness, money, and a child with a drug problem. But, he said, "God is good. Every time I want to run into a cave of self-pity, God sends me another drunk to help. I can't be lost in myself if I am doing service work." He is a beautiful example of how God works in us to reach out to us.

God is more than his involvement with us humans. If there were no humans, there would still be God. For those of us in recovery, God is forever more a verb than a noun. For those who follow a spiritual map, God is the beating, functioning foundation of our hope and existence. We can't afford to fall into the trap of intellectualizing God, for to do so is to die. Avoiding death is a powerful motivator once we have seen even a glimmer of the light that recovery brings.

THE DOOR OF THE DAMAGED HEART OPENS

For us, God not only is, but does; God not only does, but does for us. God motivated by unconditional love sends us right back where we came from to make a difference, to touch a life that was broken as ours once was. And because of that broken-ness, we know as no others do where lies the hidden, barricaded door of the damaged heart.

God not only does for us, but goes a step farther. He then asks that we allow him to work through us so we can be there for others. We use the term *service* to describe our response to that fierce call for help from our suffering brothers and sisters. Service is the very heartbeat of recovery. Service forces us to go outside of ourselves, and therein lies its power. At a recent AA/Al-Anon retreat, I found recovery at its best. Love seemed to hum everywhere. Such is the music of recovery. Let me tell you a bit about that retreat:

BLOCKED FROM THE LIGHT

The closing speaker of the retreat was Fin. He shared his story of the miracle of recovery. Through a moment of awakening, he told us, "The Voice of God hummed in my heart and head." In the past thirty-plus years, I've heard countless stories in meetings of the Voice reaching through rock, melting what we thought could never be melted, and rescuing lives that had been long given up on. It is this Voice that found us at the bottom and led us to the light.

You know the stories. They are all about love blocked, then the call, the Voice of God, and our gradual return to life stage by stage, level by level. These stories—as diverse as the recovering people who share them—show what happens before that Voice of God is heard.

- He regained consciousness strapped to a bed in a mental ward. For over ten years, he had pumped every drug he could find into his body and watered those drugs with alcohol. He thought he was a big man on the street, but he was found, snot frozen to his face, lying in a pool of urine, helpless and hopeless. He didn't look so tough or in control strapped to that bed. It was his sixteenth birthday.
- He was a celebrity, a world-renowned musician. Tens of thousands came to his concerts, cheered and shouted his name. Then, back in his room, behind the facade of celebrity, he crawled around on his hands and knees, picking up lint hoping it was a speck of cocaine. Completely by accident, he glimpsed his reflection in a mirror as he crawled around the floor like a starving animal. His reflection in that mirror pushed his self-disgust lower than he ever thought possible.
- Her first drunk was at age five, when she drained the little puddle of booze left in the bottom of a bottle. It gave her wings to fly away from the misery she felt even then. Misery born of abject poverty, alcoholic parents, and the hole in her heart she somehow knew would never be filled. For the next twenty years, she used alcohol to escape even as she fell further and further into the darkness. She evolved from being a victim to becoming a brutal bully. She hated everyone because she saw them through the lens of self that festered with violent self-hatred. If life was war, she was going to shoot first and not give a damn

who shot back. She felt she had died a long time ago, anyway, so what was there to lose?

- He had promised his four-year-old son he would be home for his birthday party. Even through his insanity, he knew he loved his son. He was sure he never intended to hurt anyone, especially his son. But he couldn't help himself. He was powerless as long as he depended on his power alone. Not surprisingly, he never made it to the birthday party. Late that night, when he staggered home and went into his son's bedroom, he saw three dried tear tracks on his son's sleeping face. He somehow knew that these tears seared all the way down to the boy's heart. As drunk as he was, he knew what he had done. His heart exploded. No words could describe the depth of his self-loathing as he stood there, looking at his son's adoring, betrayed face.

You know these stories. The people are all different, yet they all tell the same story.

SPIRITUALLY HOMELESS NO MORE

Before recovery, the afflicted and the affected, including us, are homeless in the deepest sense. We are spiritually homeless. We are lost until the coming of the Voice of God. When we start to hear the Voice of God, no matter how lost to the light we may have been, incredible, unexpected things begin happening. They surprise and dazzle us as we slowly adjust to the light.

We in recovery come to speak of amazing spiritual events like these:

- Conversion experiences. Some are white-light experiences beyond any rational explanation. Some are slower, more subdued, but nonetheless real

and powerful. Through the power of those experiences, there begins a gradual shifting from
self-centeredness to God-centeredness, from self-
reliance to God-reliance. Then, all of a sudden, we
blink our eyes and realize we are in a different place.
We may wonder how this wonderful movement happened, but somehow, somewhere, we know God is
behind it all, orchestrating the dance of our lives.

- We find ourselves surrendering where all we did before was resist. What an amazing change surrender
brings. We choose to surrender to a Higher Power so
that we do not have to depend solely on our own inadequate power, which has failed us time and time
again.

- We find ourselves letting go. Incredible relief is the
result. The burden is lifted when we no longer fanta-
size about lifting the weight alone.

- The more we become aware of God, the less fear,
worry, rage, and grief run our lives. We slowly come
to embrace spirituality as a way of life we could never
imagine in the dark, old days. Others may find these
words pious, pie-in-the-sky wishes. But for us, it is a
growing, daily occurrence. Living a spiritual life, we
become capable of what before was impossible.

- Prayer and meditation is sought. And when we stop
to listen and reflect and open our hearts and minds,
a loving, forgiving face is revealed that perhaps we
never did or could know before. We are now more
able to understand, embrace, and allow ourselves to
accept the unbelievable fact that, for reasons known
only to God, he has chosen to come to us as a friend,
not as a condemning judge.

- Family reconciliation often happens in miraculous
ways. The words "I love you" are spoken between

stone hearts melted in the fire of God's voice calling us out of darkness.

- A sense of belonging happens through community. Look at the faces around your group and reflect on the stories. Here is fellowship. And it is ours. Perhaps for the first time, we experience others *wanting* us to sit by them. Miraculously, we see faces light up when we walk in the door. We finally start to feel that we belong.

- We have been chosen to carry the message of hope to others who are as desperate and lost as we once were. God will send others across our path who somehow, quite by accident or coincidence, just happened to be there at the right time and place. Our actions will enable these people to take a step further into recovery. Slowly, we develop the sensitivity to hear the music of God's voice "in all our affairs."

OUR INNER EMPTINESS IS SUDDENLY FILLED

Amazing spiritual events allow a transformation to take place. This transformation happens within us as we allow God to fill our inner emptiness. This emptiness was initially created by love denied and love blocked. In turn, this emptiness begins to get filled by love found.

God is serious about those still suffering with addiction. He reaches out to them as he once reached out to us. He does this by reaching behind their delusion and denial in ways we could never imagine. All anyone in recovery has to do to see how tricky God is, is reflect on his or her own story. How tricky was God in pursuit of you?

It is an amazing realization to wake up to the fact that now it is our turn. Now God is using us to do his magic tricks. We may not think we have much to offer. We may feel absolutely certain that God surely has better messengers than us in doing his work. We may ask with all sincerity, "Me? A messenger sent by God to have a hand in bringing others to the light?" Yes, you. God keeps asking us to just show up and let him do his magic and stop asking so many questions. We don't have to know exactly what to do. We just have to show up and get out of the way.

Like a Glove

God knows how to use us best. It's kind of like a glove. Imagine all the different kinds of gloves there are. There are driving gloves, boxing gloves, work gloves, rubber gloves, fashionable gloves to be worn to parties, winter gloves, infection-control gloves, and gardening gloves. The list could go on and on.

Each design is specifically crafted to provide a different service. But until a hand is put into the gloves, they are just things, inanimate and useless objects, no matter how ingenious their design. Gloves are nothing without a hand filling them, bringing to completion the purpose for which they were made.

Perhaps it is not too far a stretch to see the Voice of God as a hand filling the gloves that we are. Each of us can be viewed as a glove intended for a purpose. We realize that each of us has our own beauty and integrity, but we need a hand to bring it to life.

Who better than a stumbler can touch another stumbler? Who better than one who has been in prison to speak and connect with someone else who has been incarcerated and thinks he or she is beyond recall? Who but someone who has had a hand in destroying a family can sneak into the heart of another who suffers just that guilt and shame? We are all gloves designed for specific purposes. We are the gloves that our tricky God uses to sneak behind locked and barred doors. There is no recovery without spirituality. There is no spirituality without service. There is no service if we do not show up saying: "I'll go with you, God. Use me as you will. Whatever of me it is that you can use, do it. I offer it to you."

The problem, of course, is that considering where we have been, how could that ever be turned to anything good? But then we come to understand it is the greatest gift that we have to bring to the party.

As this hand of God begins filling the glove—us, no matter how lost to the light we may have been—all manner of incredible things begin happening.

THE GREATEST GIFT

One of the clearest signs of our moving into God as God moves into us is when we find ourselves thanking God for whatever pains, terrors, and sorrows we may have endured. We thank him because as we move deeper into our own spirituality, the more committed we become to service. We want and need to reach out to others as others reached out to us. And in our deepening compliance with the spiritual principles of our program, we begin to understand that our greatest strength was forged in our worst pain and suffering. It was precisely those "worst times" that hollowed out a space in us that wouldn't have existed otherwise. And this space becomes the haven where others find the compassion, understanding, and strength we so badly needed ourselves at one time.

We have all lived in a haunted house, and as a result, we are not scared of the ghosts of others. Precisely because of that familiarity with "the worst," we acquire the key to that dimension of another. The ghosts of others aren't any worse than ours. That's how it was with Tom and Mark.

Tom just turned thirty, lives at the Union Gospel Mission, and has just celebrated his ninety-day sober birthday. He is full of hope, not only for himself but also for his daughter, whom he gets to see on weekends. His hope is that with ongoing recovery, he will be able to gain custody of her. Tom has had a tough life. He has never been taught how to love himself or anyone else. Mark knew that.

Mark is an older man who pays back the debt of having been given the program by serving as a sponsor to the men at the Mission. Mark knows all about standing in that dark place, yearning to enter the light but having no idea how to do it. Because Mark had been there, he knew what Tom was going through. Mark saw Tom hiding there in the same shadows he used to cower in. He knew where those shadows were and how bad they hurt. He reached out to Tom with that connection that goes beyond friendship and fellowship. Mark went into the darkness and got Tom. In essence, Mark refathered Tom by teaching him the meaning of honesty, trust, caring about self and others, and giving back. Mark did this gradually, of course. If you have stood long in the dark, the light is terrifying. One night, Mark asked Tom out to dinner. He said he'd pick him up at six o'clock at the front door of the Mission.

Of course, Tom didn't expect Mark to show up. He thought surely he would forget or have something else more important to do. He explained how odd it was to wait by the door for Mark with a knot in his stomach and legs trembling. Tom was sure he wasn't important enough for Mark to bother with. But Mark was even more sure he'd rather drop dead than stand the young man up. He picked him up promptly at six o'clock as promised.

At dinner, Tom told Mark how scared he was not of the dark, but the light. He told Mark he had the worst urge to use the weekend before while he was with his daughter. As much as he loved the little girl, the thought of being with someone he didn't know all that well (Mark) and doing things he didn't have a clue about (going out to dinner like a normal person) frightened him beyond words. Looking deeply into Mark's eyes, Tom said he would have relapsed except he kept thinking someone had asked him out to dinner so maybe he was worth something. Mark knew what he was talking about. Mark told Tom: "The program isn't a gift. It is a debt. Everything I give you was first given to me, and in your time, you will pass it on to another." Tom couldn't believe he would ever have anything anyone else would want, let alone need. Mark told him, "Just be patient."

In truth, the wounded serve best in this war because only they know where the wound is. We bring to service the compassion and wisdom learned from pain. Pain becomes power when held up to grace.

REACHING BACK TO OTHERS

Recovery happens in life, not in books. It is an experience to be lived, not a theory to be understood. Recovery is the experience of allowing God to slowly but steadily fill our lives, level by level and stage by stage, so that we may be of service in the healing of others who suffer still. This spiritual impulse to reach back to others was beautifully described by General William Booth, founder of the Salvation Army. He said, "While women weep as they do now, I'll fight; while children go hungry as they do now, I'll fight; while men go to prison, in and out, in and out, I'll fight; while there remains one dark soul without the light of God I'll fight—I'll fight to the very end."

Now there passes a man worth walking with.

WHAT WORKS

Twelve Step practitioners find the Voice of God clearly expressed in the spiritual principles our program is founded upon. Principles are clear statements of what works as gleaned from our own experiences and those of the giants who have gone before us. One of these principles is that our Higher Power, the God of our understanding, cares for us. That is why in the Third Step we are told to surrender ourselves into the "care of God." Not into the power of God or the intelligence of God, but into the care of God.

No matter how long it takes to be able to even understand what *care* might be, let alone *trust*, it is our saving principle. It shows that indeed there is a Higher Power, and that Power cares about us.

The payoff for whatever effort it may take to be able to hear the Voice of this God is to form a connection with this God. We make contact. We grow into the understanding that spirituality is not about some part of our lives; it is about the content of our entire lives.

QUESTIONS

1. Why is recovery fundamentally about my spirituality?
2. Why does spirituality always take me back to the question of intimacy?
3. When are three times I have clearly heard the "Voice of God" in my recovery?

MOVING ON TO CHAPTER 5

Spread before us is an overview of our map of recovery to joy and abundance. The map shows the area that must be traveled. The map shows where rough traveling exists as we move through the various stages of our spiritual blockage. But it also shows the reason for all this effort and the help we can expect with every step we take. It's time to connect those dots.

CHAPTER 5

Connecting the Dots: Road Signs along the Map of Recovery

~

Only we are responsible for our recovery. Accepting that responsibility requires us to make the effort to learn how to connect the dots on our map of recovery.

The reason for the content and the positioning of this chapter at the end of Section 1 is solely to provide a review of the ideas we have covered so far. It's also a heartfelt plea for you to spend the time and energy necessary to integrate these ideas into your own life. This is the process of connecting the dots.

WHY INTEGRATION TRANSLATES INTO WISDOM

The idea of this chapter is to integrate all we've learned in the previous Section 1 chapters into our understanding of our own recovery. Integration is an essential concept used in this book. In this context, integration can be defined as chewing on the material we've covered so far, taking it apart, and discussing it. Only after we reach that point can we gain wisdom from this material. To help us with our integration, in addition to the suggested discussion questions found at the conclusion of the chapter, you will find "As It Applies to Your Life" sections in the middle of this chapter. By taking the time to answer these questions honestly, you will begin to understand what you've learned so far by reading this book in the context of your own recovery and life experiences. You will discover the truth. The only truth any of us can use is our own truth. The only way someone else's truth can eventually become our truth is by integrating it into our lives. We can do this by learning a new truth at a meeting, through reading a book, or through some other experience. A truth isn't ours until we make it ours by fully understanding and accepting it. At that point, nobody can take it from us.

UNDERSTANDING IS KEY

A major benefit of the recovery map and spiritual/human model of recovery presented here in Section 1 is that it provides an understanding of why both positive and negative consequences happen in our lives. In truth, beliefs are the cookie cutters of our lives. Negative beliefs, the old lies, always lead to negative consequences. Positive beliefs, the new truths, always lead to positive consequences. A cookie cutter shaped like a Santa Claus will never make a cookie that looks like a Christmas tree. We need to develop an understanding of what cookie cutter to use in order to deliver the shape of cookie we want.

Only by understanding the benefit of cause and effect can we learn to connect the dots in our lives. Taking the time and energy to understand how the dots connect in our own lives is the price we pay to gain control of our lives. It's worth the effort. I derive immense satisfaction from seeing the light go on in people's eyes as they connect the dots in their own lives. I can still hear them shout, "I get it! I finally get it! I finally understand who is driving my bus!"

Getting to this point of understanding is not always easy

for a number of reasons. To start, it's impossible without a map to follow. Another reason people tend not to put in the effort of integration is because our society doesn't much value connecting dots of any kind. We are far more likely to be impulsive than try to understand what we did and what the consequences will be later. It takes too much time. Instead, we worship speed. We demand instant communication, instant coverage of world events, instant gratification, instant wealth, and even instant relationships. Ultimately, even fast food isn't fast enough—we want instant food.

What is lost in our fast-paced society is depth. What is lost is not only the chance to reflect on our stories, but even the thought that we should *want* to reflect on them. In turn, what is lost is wisdom. Wisdom and connecting the dots demand spending the time it takes to reflect on what we learn. And if we don't learn, how will we ever go forward? How will we ever learn to create new tomorrows rather than just repeat a thousand yesterdays? That is why integration is so crucial.

As explained earlier, the following "test questions" are provided to give us a chance to review some of the concepts we've learned so far as they apply to our own recovery and life experiences.

I have always believed that the best way to learn anything is to teach it. Only when we try to teach something do we understand what we don't understand. The following questions are written in a format that can be used within a group discussion, if you'd like. I suggest taking turns teaching the following process point by point to each other to derive maximum benefit from reading this book. When we try to teach others, we learn mighty fast that we don't understand quite as much as we thought we did. Ample time should be given to explain the reasoning behind each response. We can connect the dots by explaining to others what causes the consequences in our lives and why the dots are what they are in the first place. Each set of questions in the "As It Applies to Your Life" sections help us get started. When we share our answers to these questions with others, we can all benefit from the feedback of others. As a result of sharing how this model unfolds in our lives, everyone gains a richer understanding and depth of the spiritual/human model of recovery in our lives. You don't need a group to get something out of this chapter, but it is how the greatest good will be gained.

If you are unable to answer these questions about yourself and your recovery at this time for whatever reason, know that they are here. Know that if and when the time comes for you to "take that next step," the map showing you where you are going and why the road leads us as it does is here waiting for you. Rewards often come in proportion to the risk taken. Imagine the loss if you had failed to attend your first meeting because of the incredible jitters that you might have experienced.

A short summary of the key points presented in previous chapters is included here in sequential order. There is a reason why we start with the importance of learning to honor our story and then move in an orderly and understandable fashion through the rest of the material covered in Section 1. One insight builds upon the next. This makes the most sense. It is most beneficial if each step is understood as coming from the one before it and leading up to the next one. I encourage you to take your time in answering these questions.

KEY POINT 1: As we saw in chapter 1, we must learn to honor our story.

Our lives are the only stories we have. Our story is us. It is either within our own story that we find God and recovery, or we will never find it. There is no such thing as virtual recovery. We can't live our recovery through anyone else, no matter how marvelous we may think their story is. The fact is no one's story is better than ours. We are all given our own stage to dance on as best we can. Who is to say one is better than the other? We don't know anyone else's heart any more than they know ours. Our experiences are as important and valuable as anyone else's. Accepting this truth puts us well on our way to abundance and joy.

- *As It Applies to Your Life:* What was the condition of your life before you began recovery? What is the condition of your life now? How great a distance is there between where you began and where you are now? What breakthroughs have you experienced in your recovery? How congratulatory would you be of someone in your group who had made as much progress as you have? Why isn't your progress as wonderful as theirs?

KEY POINT 2: As we saw in chapter 2, every human being is born with the need for love and belonging.

All human beings are born with the need for intimacy and belonging. The hunger for the fulfillment of those needs is at the core of our humanity. Though we were born with these needs, none of us was born with the skills to meet those needs. How we learn to meet those needs depends on brain chemistry, birth order, genetics, culture, and random luck. Among the most powerful of those components is family programming. Much of who we are and how we are was learned in our early family formation. We all learned there were rules on how or if we were to get the "good stuff" our hearts were made for.

- *As It Applies to Your Life:* What were the rules you learned about getting love and acceptance? Did what you learn make you "strong" or "weak"? What made you "good" or "bad"? Clearly state the "old lie" you learned about yourself in these formative experiences. Remember to connect the "old lie" with the driving need to fulfill the basic, spiritual needs.

KEY POINT 3: In chapter 2, we also saw how tenacious the acting out of that "old lie" is. We keep carrying the old perceptions of the past into the present.

Every human being ever born set out immediately, learning even in infancy, what the "rules" were to get the "good stuff." Was the world safe? Am I safe? What do I have to do to be accepted? Can I trust that the same response will come from the same behavior? Is the world predictable? Am I good enough to be loved? Is it safe to be vulnerable? "What we live with we learn. What we learn we practice. What we practice we become. What we become has consequences" *(Stage II Recovery: Life beyond Addiction)*.

Countless people learn early on that they and life are not safe and that they should never trust. The best coping technique is to con, manipulate, and lie—anything is better than being vulnerable. The truth is that successful relationships require vulnerability. If you lack the ability to trust, you are forever sentenced to isolation. The constant sabotaging of relationships is the result.

Without a clue of what healthy negotiation through conflict might look or feel like, successful relationships are again impossible. People cheated of this critical life management skill simply repeat the violent or otherwise failed negotiation techniques witnessed as children with the same results. Successful participation in healthy relationships is the only way to meet their hearts' deepest need.

Life is not just difficult; it is dangerous. So many of us experienced abuse at the most fragile time in our lives (infancy and childhood). Because of this, our personalities, perceptions, traits, expectations, and beliefs make it impossible to share in the "good stuff." This failure creates a terrible spiritual vacuum that we try to fill with all kinds of things except what works.

- *As It Applies to Your Life:* Have you ever experienced difficulty dealing with intimacy? How have you consistently acted when intimacy comes into your life? How do the dots connect between the "rules" you identified in the first set of questions and your consistent behavior relative to relationships? How is your "then" still your "now"?

KEY POINT 4: As we saw in chapter 3, everyone in recovery has Stage II work to do.

Every human being has life work to do in order to live well. Life work is about understanding what the "lie" we internalized from our earliest years is, how it is still functioning in our lives, and how to reverse the power of that self-defeating pattern. Recovery demands we do this work. For us, this life work—what we call Stage II Recovery—is not a luxury. It is a necessity. There is no such thing as maintenance in recovery. We are on a greased pole. We either climb or slide backward.

- *As It Applies to Your Life:* How might you connect your self-defeating behaviors (the practice, to habit, to reality) with your understanding of the "searching and fearless" nature of your Fourth Step? How might your new understanding of this "negative process" relate to your understanding of the nature of what you share in your Fifth Step? How might the presence of this deeply ingrained pattern in your life relate to the meaning of the first three steps: "I can't, he can, so I'll let him"? Can't what? Let him do what?

KEY POINT 5: We also saw in chapter 3 that in recovery we must go to the level of the damage we have sustained (by the experiences of learning our old lie). For some, the damage goes all the way to the bone. It bloodies the deepest levels of our being.

Everyone has been hurt and has a sad story to tell, but not everyone has the same dragon prowling just behind his or her eyes. Some are hurt on deeper levels than others and are the victims of the ongoing legacy of abuse—we call recovery from such abuse Stage III work. Those people need to "go as deep as the damage is" if they are to experience their fair share of joy and abundance in their lives.

Not everyone needs to do Stage III work—on the level where abuse has done its deadly work—because not everyone in recovery carries what we call "the legacy of abuse." But where it is present, it must be addressed.

- *As It Applies to Your Life:* How do you define Stage I Recovery in your life? Explain the meaning of Stage II Recovery in your life. Does Stage III Recovery apply to you? Why or why not? Explain what all three levels have to do with your "old lie" and what you were trying to gain when it was imprinted in your soul. Connect the dots.

KEY POINT 6: As we saw in chapter 4, God is the glue that holds us together because God is love and learning to love is recovery. God is the road we travel on and the fuel that carries us along that road in recovery. There is not recovery at any stage or level without conscious contact with the God of our understanding.

- *As It Applies to You:* What role has God played in your recovery? Express specific times when you heard the Voice of God directing you. Cite an example of when God took care of you in a unique, personal way in your recovery. What do you believe is "God's will" for you?

Have you connected the dots? The point of these "test questions" is for you to see the connection between the dots in your life. The following diagram is given to help you understand more and give a recap of the human/spiritual model of recovery.

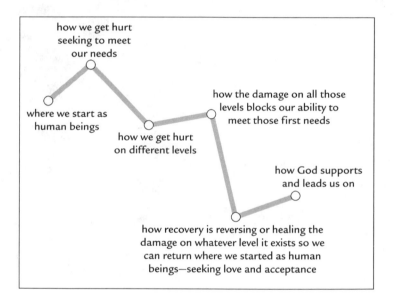

how we get hurt
seeking to meet
our needs

where we start as
human beings

how we get hurt
on different levels

how the damage on all those
levels blocks our ability to
meet those first needs

how God supports
and leads us on

how recovery is reversing or healing the
damage on whatever level it exists so we
can return where we started as human
beings—seeking love and acceptance

QUESTIONS

1. What have you learned about your own recovery by reviewing Key Points 1–6?
2. Who is responsible for your recovery?
3. Are you starting to be able to connect the dots in your recovery?

MOVING ON TO CHAPTER 6

It is time to take a deeper, closer look at the various elements of our map. It is time to move on. In Section 2, we take a more detailed look at the various stages spelled out on the map as well as the abundance and joy we are moving steadily toward.

The Stages of Recovery

CHAPTER 6

Stage I Recovery:
Sobriety First—
Arresting the Addiction

～

Achieving sobriety is always the first step for any recovering addict. This is Stage I Recovery. For an addict, it is always sobriety first. For an addict, every good thing in life begins with sobriety.

I struggled with how to write this chapter. The difficulty was not having too little to say, but rather too much. The subject of this chapter, as with all the others, is so rich, so deep, and so mysterious that its reality played out in the real world overwhelms any words used to express or describe it. Simply put, Stage I Recovery is arresting the addiction. The miracle of arresting an addiction is obvious to anyone who looks into the face of a person suffering an active addiction. Stage I Recovery is not an enemy of Stage II Recovery, but rather its foundation.

THE MYSTERY AND THE MIRACLE

How could we who have experienced separation from our addiction be anything but overwhelmed by the mystery and magnitude of the power of addiction and the equal miracle of recovery? The longer we are around recovery, if we keep our heads in the game, the more astounding it becomes. What

words could adequately express the miracle of watching someone poisoned by lethal addiction turn his or her life around and
begin a new life based on gratitude and service? What words are
powerful enough to illuminate the miracle of a life eaten by
guilt, shame, and hopeless addiction that then reverses itself
and begins, step-by-step, to build a cathedral where once only
devastation existed? What words are bright enough to paint the
picture of a woman so lost to alcoholism that she lost her children and scarcely knew they were gone? But then, the miracle
happened. That miracle was Stage I Recovery. Now, thirty-
seven years later, all seven of her children show up for her
medallion night with nothing but love and admiration in their
hearts.

SOBRIETY FIRST

I simply have no words to express the importance and wonder
of "sobriety first." The importance of Stage II Recovery, dealing
with life after sobriety, in no way diminishes the crucial necessity of achieving sobriety—Stage I Recovery. The critical importance and miracle of first arresting the addiction is obvious to
anyone who understands how powerful, cunning, and baffling
alcoholism truly is. Consider Sue's story. Sue is a recovering alcoholic but claims her deeper addiction is gambling. She also is
addicted to new, hot relationships. Even though she is currently
in a satisfying long-term relationship, the lure to stray, to find
"the hot sauce," as she names it, is always a pull. She got up at
her meeting saying our tried-and-true line: "We are only as sick
as our secrets." She had a secret she needed to share no matter
how much guilt and shame she felt.

About a month ago, she heard about a contest on the radio.
It was a game of chance, a drawing. Her engines began to fire.
Sue had tried every kind of drug there was, but what tasted the
sweetest to her was a full-blown adrenaline rush. Sue loved the

buzz. She loved the jolt. She loved the rockets going off in her head when she was on the edge.

Sue knew she had what she called her "crazy uncle chained up in her basement." He could be quiet for a while, but sooner or later he always went kind of psycho and tried to break out. She knew she could not be around any activity that required chance or skill to win. There was no winning for her in these events. There was only loss. There was only the crazy part of her trying to break free and jump off some cliff. She knew all that, but she went ahead anyway. She failed to do the next right thing. Her engines were on a low rumble.

Sue told us she didn't call her sponsor, she didn't get to a meeting, and she didn't do the prayer and meditation of an Eleventh Step. She willingly let her addiction lead her into the terrible darkness. Besides the seductive lure of winning a contest, she said the voice of the announcer sounded "yummy." That sensation also was a red flag screaming at her to do the next right thing—which, again, she didn't.

Sure enough, she justified why she was going to call the radio station: "Not that I was going to get involved, of course, but just to see who the announcer was and how the contest was going to be run." Now on the other side of this dangerous near miss, Sue hung her head as she talked to us. The announcer "just happened to be available," and wouldn't you know, he seemed to like her voice as much as she liked his. Her engine was open full throttle now. They established a place to meet where they could "discuss the contest." She then explained, "It wasn't the contest we were going after. We both knew it. He didn't care. But somehow I did."

And so, with all the adrenaline and pizzazz of her dual addiction stoking the fire, Sue said she had one last moment of sanity before she slipped down the well and lost all that she had worked so hard to build. Her engines were redlining at this point, but she said that something even more powerful, for whatever reason, was also pounding the path of her soul. In her last sane moment, something of grace came to her, and she reached out to it. Whether it was God or not, she wasn't sure. She explained that "something almighty, good, and bright was keeping me afloat. I ran like a crazy person to my sponsor, who met me before the meeting I had been skipping, and it saved my ass." Sue dodged a bullet. There are only so many times a person can successfully do that. She recognized that "my addiction is as sneaky as it is patient. It is perverse and lives an inch beneath my skin. I need to always keep an eye on it or I'm gone."

Can you relate to Sue's "sneaky, patient, and perverse" addiction, which is living "an inch beneath the skin"? You know the stories. If you are now in recovery, you know the ugliness, tragedy, and sadness of an active addiction. Therefore, you also know the supreme necessity and glory of sobriety won. It simply is not possible to overestimate the importance of sobriety.

THE MYSTERY AT THE HEART OF THE MIRACLE

Addictions cannot be outthought, outrun, or outfoxed. They cannot be silenced or hidden. Addictions are cannibals whose appetite is only satisfied when they have eaten their host, whole and entire. Addictions prey on every defense set to oppose them except one. Addictions can only be arrested through surrender to the recovery process, stage by stage, inch by inch, whole and entire. That is the mystery at the heart of the miracle.

Only a truly profound conversion experience has ever been proven to possess the power necessary to halt the ruthless rampage of an addiction that, by its nature, is bent on destroying the life it afflicts. Conversion experiences, by their very definition, are spiritual. Spiritual experiences happen to us, but they do not come from us.

A STORY OF VICTORY AFTER RELAPSE

Why, then, do some "make it" and so many others do not? How is it that some, certainly no better or more deserving than others, are gifted with this surrender experience and others are not? Of course, relapse happens when we get sloppy and dishonest with our program. That is not the question. The question is, "When so much is at stake and surrender has apparently happened, why would anyone get sloppy and dishonest with what saves them?"

Last week at an open meeting, Chris shared a brilliant account of how subtle the disease of alcoholism is in his life and what it took for genuine recovery to begin. Chris was given his three-year medallion at this meeting. Chris said he started going to meetings because he was being threatened by his wife. He felt that he didn't really have a problem. At the end of the first meeting, the old-timers just smiled, hugged him, and told him to keep coming back. He went out and used.

The next time around, he told the old-timers he guessed he might need these meetings, but he wasn't about to "go overboard." He said he would never arrive early, he'd leave right after the meeting was over, and he'd just put in his time until he was cured. Again, the old-timers smiled, hugged him, and told him to keep coming back. They knew. Chris went out and used again.

After more missed meetings, Chris returned. He decided the answer to his alcohol problem this time was in the science of recovery. He researched the founding of the program, learned all the important names, and compared the "science of AA" with other philosophies. Once again, the old-timers smiled, hugged him, and told him to keep coming back. They knew. Chris went out and used again.

Next time around, Chris decided God was the answer to his problems—though not the "God of our understanding," but the God of his convenience, or, as Chris put it, "The God of my head, not my heart." He went on: "God without working the program is like a lightbulb without electricity. The bulb is there, but not the juice to make it work." Chris said this time the old-timers hugged him even tighter and told him to keep coming back. They knew. After discovering that this God of convenience was far too frail to sustain him in his fight against addictions, he went out and used again.

Finally, he came back eternally amazed at and grateful for all the chances he had been given. There he stood, three years later, humbled and steeped in the true wisdom of the program. Finally, he was gratefully sober and truly getting it. "Now," Chris says, "I come early and stay late. I listen and learn. And I hug the new guys and tell them to keep coming back." What sets Chris apart from all those people who are still out there actively suffering in their addiction? What else is there to say but recovery is a mystery and a miracle?

SURRENDER TO WIN

Miracles can't be explained; they can only be experienced, observed, and learned from. Seeing the miracle of surrender pervade a life is a miracle in itself. That is one reason why everyone in the Twelve Step program is among the most blessed of human beings. Surrender is moving from reliance on our own power to reliance on a Higher Power. It is the giving in and giving up on the idea that the alcoholic can drink like anyone else. It's all there in the Big Book on pages 32–33: "[they] fell victim to a belief which practically every alcoholic has—that his long period of sobriety and self-discipline had qualified him to drink as other men. . . . Most of us have believed that if we remained sober for a long stretch, we could thereafter drink normally. . . . If we are planning to stop drinking, there must be no reservation of any kind, nor any lurking notion that someday we will be immune to alcohol." Surrender is doing what we need to do to climb back into the ranks of humanity. Surrender is grace. This grace is the only road anyone has yet found to quality recovery.

The Big Book tells us "half measures avail us nothing." Never is this truer than in the realm of the final, total, complete surrender of one's life to one's Higher Power, the God of our understanding. And as we get better, we find our God gets better. As the mud comes off our window, the sun shines more brightly. If we want a better God, we need to be better people. The Big Book tells us gaining the "happy road of recovery" requires that we submit "all of our affairs" to the power of practicing the spiritual principles of the program. Whatever we will not own and hold up cannot be healed. Whatever insanity, guilt, fear, shame, resentment, and rage we hide in the dark will devour us. Whatever spiritual thief we let roam our house will steal our souls. God demands it all. We cannot give it all until we are willing to throw open the guilt-rusted, shame-rusted, fear-rusted, rage-rusted last door that we refuse to surrender. That is why the God of recovery keeps after us and keeps hammering on those barricaded doors in our souls. God keeps vigil before our locked door, patiently waiting for us to open it, if just a crack, so he can come pouring in like a new dawn.

The Big Book calls alcoholism "powerful, cunning, and baffling." Many would add something else—patient. This patient, fatal disease is just waiting for an opening. How many people have you known who, after a spell, got sloppy with their program? They played with it. They failed to take it seriously. They put their heads in the mouth of the tiger one too many times and found out too late the fangs were still there. Never underestimate the power of your disease. We are more than our disease, but we dare not forget that we as addicts can never again use with impunity. The only reprieve from being destroyed by our disease is the daily surrender of our will to the Power greater than ourselves.

Willard, my steadfast partner in recovery, who has nearly forty years of uninterrupted sobriety, once put it this way to me: "When an alcoholic drinks, it is like dancing with a five-hundred-pound gorilla. You may get tired and want to stop, but the gorilla always wants to keep on dancing. And the gorilla always gets what he wants." That seemed to say it pretty well.

LET GO OF THE ROPE, SWEETIE

Marilyn is over fifty years old now. She grew up on a farm where the girls were as expected to toss bales of hay and fix tractors as the boys were. Marilyn could outthrow and outwork any of her brothers. She did it to attract her father's attention, but it never worked. Her father only wanted sons. Her original sin was being born female.

She walked off the farm decades ago, but looking at her hardy, rough exterior, you know the farm never left her. Marilyn's ancestors were all alcoholics, including her father. She married an alcoholic and drank addictively herself for twenty-five years. Fifteen years ago, she found a shaky sobriety. She was dry and grateful but far from peaceful. Marilyn relapsed often in those first years. She'd plow ahead with her program, then be so overtaken with feelings of inadequacy, sadness, and rage she couldn't stand it. After relapsing, she persevered by continuing to work the Steps as persistently as she worked on the farm as a child. She truly was grateful; she just wasn't very peaceful. Somehow, the terrible wounds of her abiding sense of rejection, failure, and inadequacy from her youth never left her. She couldn't shake the broken-glass feeling of never having been accepted or, as far as she could tell, loved by her father.

But then the divine father she calls God came and got her.

As she talked about this experience, her tired, rough face changed. A light of innocence appeared. It was as if a child was emerging, fresh and innocent. For Marilyn, this experience came in the form of a dream. In her dream, she was a child living on the farm. She was holding one end of a rope that went over a bar above a deep well. The other end of the rope dangled above the open mouth of the well. That end of the rope held a huge, stinking, fetid mass of something, she said. The obvious thing to do was to let go of the rope and send it far away down the well. The problem was she couldn't let go of the rope. Something beyond her control demanded she dutifully hang on to the rope. Then the most amazing thing happened. Her father, who had been dead for thirty years, walked up to her, put his hand on her shoulder, and said, "It's okay. Let go of the rope, Sweetie." And she did. With tears in her eyes, Marilyn told us one of the fondest memories she had of her father. She couldn't remember the circumstance, but for whatever unfathomable reason, her father had called her Sweetie. It only happened once, but she never forgot.

No matter how big the enemy or how powerful the affliction, there is one answer greater than any obstacle that can stand against it: the connection with the God of our understanding. The God who comes and tells us, as he did Marilyn, it's okay. Let go of the rope. Every day, every hour, one day at a time, stage by stage and step by step—*let go of the rope.*

QUESTIONS

1. Why must recovery for an addict always begin with sobriety first?
2. Why is it true to say that sobriety is but the first step of recovery?
3. What "life work" remains for us to do once sobriety has been achieved?

MOVING ON TO CHAPTER 7

And once we have, or have even just begun to, let go of the rope, what do we find? Take alcohol out of the equation, and what we are left with is us. The world hasn't changed. It is we who must change. Now our recovery energy must focus on our lives and all the failed techniques we learned, so long ago, to cope with our problems. Now comes learning to deal with life on its own terms—Stage II Recovery.

CHAPTER 7

Stage II Recovery:
Learning to Live Life Differently

～

*Since recovery is our spiritual journey through life, after absti-
nence is achieved we must address the obstacles in our lives that
limit this ongoing recovery. Doing our "life work" is Stage II
Recovery.*

The redline on the map of recovery moving toward joy and
abundance pushes on—not *instead* of sobriety but *because* of it;
not replacing it but standing on its shoulders. After arresting
the addiction, it's time to learn how to deal with life as it is in a
new, better way. This is moving from Stage I Recovery into
Stage II Recovery.

THE TICKET THAT GETS US ON THE BUS

This stage of recovery is simply doing one's life work, which
isn't always so simple at all. Our lives, as wounded and battered
as they might be, are what's left once sobriety has been
achieved. Sobriety is the ticket that gets us on the bus. Learning to live life differently is what makes the ride worth all the
effort. And it will require some effort. If chemicals medicate
pain, sobriety leaves us once again exposed to life's pain with
no better way to cope with it than before. If we don't find that
"better way," our recovery leaves us with essentially three

options: We can either switch addictions, relapse, or white-knuckle our way to sobriety. And if we white-knuckle our recovery, we never reach the amount of abundance and joy that is possible for us.

Nothing is worse than being successful at a lie. We've said all along that our "old lies" are at the core of everything negative in our lives before, during, and after an addiction has been arrested. These lies might include beliefs like "I must be perfect; I will trust no one; I am only as good as I can produce; no one will ever love me, so why try; feelings are dangerous, so kill all feelings; if I don't get involved, I won't get hurt; if I give them what they want, maybe they will accept me; if I hide well enough, no one can find me; and life is war, so I'm going to hit them first."

At one time, the behavior we developed around these lies may have saved our lives. They may, in fact, have been our best friends. But now, at the point of being ready to begin Stage II Recovery, we make a new discovery. Those very set-in-concrete coping techniques and the lies at the center of them are the precise obstacles to our full measure of abundance and joy.

THE TIDE STOPS HERE

We know the demeaning "miserable places" that following the old lies brings us to. We know the frustration of knowing we want to be different, but not being able to do things differently. Some call these mental traps and emotional swamps we get stuck in the "ism" of alcoholism. Some call it a dry drunk. Some use other labels like codependent, shame-based, or dysfunctional. The Big Book often speaks of the alcoholic's "distorted thinking." Others get a bit more descriptive and call our twisted, impaired thinking "having rats in the head."

Whatever the name we use, we know how it feels. Think of all these acted-out negative processes as an evil tide that flows through generations of people. It comes down to us from those who went before. This tide is made of addictions never arrested, character defects gone unchecked, issues never dealt with, fears, rages, guilt, grief, and sadness never faced. This tide picks up speed and power with every generation. Unchallenged at each generational checkpoint, the tide rolls on until it comes to our door. If we fail to stem the tide now, it will flow through us as well, infecting those precious others who follow us, who count on us to show them a better way.

Stage II Recovery is about standing up and declaring, "It stops here!" Here we take our stand against whatever evil may have come to us down the long corridor of our history. Last week at a Sunday recovery service, a tough, shaved-head, tattooed young man lovingly escorted his six-year-old daughter for communion. Henry was now two months into recovery. His mother (the child's grandmother) immediately followed behind the two of them. She had just celebrated her first sober year. Mother and son had taken their stand and declared, "It stops here!" And the innocent little girl walked comfortably in front of her dad in absolute certainty that she would be protected and loved.

WHEN DO WE "GET THERE"?

Yet the question always is, "How do we do the work of 'stopping it here'?" How do we take our stand? Without a map, how do we even know where "here" is? Keep in mind that there are many in recovery who do not want to do any more than they have already done in their recovery. This is fine. My message here is for those on the recovery road who do feel a need to "go further." Someone is knocking at the door. Many of us come to that door knowing we are continually making the same disastrous decisions as before, which continually lead to disastrous consequences. We are grateful for the gifts recovery has brought us in the past, but are eager for more freedom, strength, joy, and compassion. Yet the questions always are, "How do we do this work? How do we take our stand in the narrow pass of our present lives even if we are willing?"

Once again, do you recall a time on your recovery path where something happened, you hit a speed bump along the way, and an event triggered a ton of "old stuff"? You may have thought, "I dealt with all that years ago. I thought I was done with all that!" As one woman put it, "When will I finally get the word *recovered* stamped on me like a side of beef?" Wrong questions have no right answers. Wondering, let alone agonizing over, when we will finally "get there" comes from seeing recovery as an event (achieving sobriety) and not a process or journey. It's essentially a spiritual journey. There is no end or "been there, done that." All there is, is better—and more—and further.

Understanding recovery in this light allows us to understand that when "old stuff" jumps up, it isn't a failure. It isn't a sign that we haven't done a good job dealing with "it" back when. What the "jumping up" does is ask us to move to a new, deeper level of our recovery. Here, the God of our understanding stands waiting for us to show up so that we may experience healing on a deeper level.

LOST IN A BLIZZARD OF LABELS

In recent years, labels have littered the field of recovery like falling leaves in October. As I travel around the country, I hear: "Hello, I'm Frank, alcoholic, chemically dependent." "Hi, I'm Joe, drug addict, rage-a-holic." "Hello, I'm Mary, alcoholic, co-dependent." "Hi, I'm Harold, chemically dependent, codependent, shame-based." "Hi, I'm Agnes, druggie, adult child, dually addicted." "Hello, I'm Eddie; I'm the king of addicts. I catch any addiction floating around."

All these labels seem to be attempts to move beyond the glorious victory of abstinence. "Yes," they seem to say, "I am an abstinent addict but I still have living problems. I need to keep going. These labels are a way of naming those problems." As good as this intention may be, it can get confusing. And confusion can be a fine place for addictions to hide. Can't you just hear someone saying, "I'm all of these labels. Who wouldn't drink with all the things that are wrong with me?"

The meaning of all these labels and how we use them can be found painted in ten-foot-high letters stating, "My problem is me!" We may say: "I have problems with relationships, with boundaries, and about being good enough. I still feel the urge to try to fill the hole within my spirit with alcohol, but I am at the center of all my problems. Something inside of me doesn't work right. Something inside of me is out of focus, if not downright broken."

Stage II Recovery work is about the "me" that stands in front of the bathroom mirror each morning. It is about getting to the cause of our problems rather than endlessly putting Band-Aids on symptoms. While putting Band-Aids on symptoms is fine (ask anyone who has ever taken an aspirin for a headache), the symptom will continue to return until the cause of the problem is figured out and acted on. That is why connecting the dots is so important in our recovery. These symptoms tend to drain away energy and attention that could be spent in happier, more productive ways.

STAGE II WORK = LIFE WORK

There is more than one way of doing Stage II Recovery work. When egos get out of control, we often tend to think we know the one and only right way of doing recovery, even though we might not know as much as we think we do or want others to think we do. A friend of mine who is a counselor at a treatment center told me how he makes the point of the alcoholic's strange combination of bloated ego and monumental insecurity. After the first few days of treatment, he calls together all the new people in treatment. He asks them if they have ever been to treatment before. Most say no. He asks them if they have ever run a treatment program before. Again, they say no. Then, he asks if any of them have ideas about how to improve the program. True to form, he says, they all know exactly how to improve the program. They don't know the questions, but they have absolute certainty regarding the answers.

Again, I'm not saying there is only one way to do Stage II work. I'm only saying our life work needs to be done if we want as much abundance and joy as is possible for us.

Let Now Be Now, Not Then

Stage II Recovery enables us to distinguish between now and then so we can let now be now and not then. Life work is always about learning to respond to the events in our present life with the emotional intensity appropriate to the event and not with the emotional intensity that was appropriate to tragic situations twenty or thirty years ago. For example, consider these situations:

- When someone cuts you off on the highway, don't look for a flamethrower to turn the driver into a cinder. That's old stuff. It's no big deal. Let it go. Get in the now.
- When people get up to leave when you are speaking at a meeting, don't get all riled up because they are discounting you. Maybe they just have to go to the bathroom. That's old stuff. It's no big deal. Let it go. Get in the now.

- When people have disagreements with you, it doesn't mean either they or you are total idiots. You don't have to write them out of your life forever. That's old stuff. It's no big deal. Let it go. Get in the now.
- When you have to wait in line, it doesn't mean you have to "get even" by making a scene. Everyone waits. Waiting is not a personal assault directed at you. That's old stuff. It's no big deal. Let it go. Get in the now.
- When someone asks you your opinion, you don't have to beat the person up with your thoughts or act like you never had a thought in your life. That's old stuff. It's no big deal. Let it go. Get in the now.

How Our Past Controls the Present

Failed recovery is responding to present-day situations with yesterday's emotional package—which you used back when the situation was totally different. Serenity or living in a state of recovery is all about letting yesterday be yesterday and today be today. Recovery is training ourselves by practicing daily disciplines to act in the present as the present and not from the emotional stance of a thousand past yesterdays. These yesterdays are long dead except where we allow them to be fully alive inside us. We can never experience the abundance and joy that is available to us by allowing yesterday to live with such terrible intensity in our hearts, minds, and bodies today. Think of every day as a new baby being born to us. Allowing the worst of yesterday to be the architect of our today is like taking that child and sacrificing it on some pagan altar of antiquity. Such a loss is tragic beyond words.

Do parts of your past control your present? Whether you

answer yes or no, see if you relate to any of the following situations.

- When we react badly to some everyday criticism, "open the trapdoor in your mind." Who is driving the bus of your life? How old is that person? What situation is he or she acting from? What is our negative present-day response really about?
- When we feel discouraged by where our capacity for intimacy has been damaged, "open the trapdoor in your mind." Who is driving the bus of your life? How old is that person? What situation is he or she acting from? What is our negative present-day response really about?
- When we fall into the trap of trying to fill the hole in our hearts with more money, more work, more sex, more stuff, "open the trapdoor in your mind." Who is driving the bus of your life? How old is that person? What situation is he or she acting from? What is our negative present-day response really about?
- When we swallow our integrity by pretending something is all right or "just fine" when it really isn't, "open the trapdoor in your mind." Who is driving the bus of your life? How old is that person? What situation is he or she acting from? What is our negative present-day response really about?
- If we allowed a five-year-old child to drive our car, how long would it be before some terrible accident happened? Five-year-old children are not able to drive a car. It would be unfair and cruel to ask a five-year-old to drive. Why would we expect anything different if we put an emotionally fixated five-year-old in charge of our lives?

We have all been affected by our past. But none of us has to be victims of our past unless we allow the evil tide to sweep us away. If we allow this to happen, we will re-create the past every day of our present lives. We then allow the past's process of pain, loss, and misery to be the blueprint of all our tomorrows.

Unchecked pain tends to fixate us at the point where our pain was first felt. Unrecognized, unchecked pain guarantees that this negative process of emotional fixation in our past will imprison us in an unending loop of disastrous thoughts, feelings, and actions. And we give that cycle of pain a free ticket to pass down to the next generation. Stage II Recovery says, "It stops here!"

It's all so clear if we only learn to connect the dots and follow the map.

REALITY IS OPTIONAL

Stage II Recovery centers on surely one of the most astounding truths a human being can discover: Reality is optional. We all must live in the house of our own reality. The incredible part is, we get to decide what that house will look like and where it is built. We do this by using the timber of our humanity, crooked though it may be, to build a life of honesty and integrity. Chuck put it this way: "I no longer plant time bombs out ahead of myself." Chuck is a member of the Life Management Program, a cutting-edge program we've been teaching for over twenty years in the United States and abroad, which shows people how to connect the dots of their recovery. Life Management provides the direction, support, and accountability to identify a participant's "old lie" and replace it with a powerful "new truth."

It's important to recognize the difference between the old lie and the new truth because there is no choice unless we see the options. We only have choices if equally available options are open to us. Only when we clearly see Road A and Road B is there a true decision about which to follow. Successful Stage II work provides the ability to see and understand the different roads (that of the old lie or the new truth), which then offers the free choice of which we will follow. After a certain point, recovery to abundance and joy is nothing more than the consistent, plodding-ahead willingness to make continual decisions based on our new reality, our new truth, and our new chosen path.

Recovery-love is the reward of the hard, courageous work we do in our lives by making those decisions daily, or multiple times a day. Recovery-love is the ability to participate in the "good stuff." And it is only through participating in this recovery-love that we are able to heal the damage that underlies all addicted lives. If we've been there, we know. What words are big enough or deep enough to adequately express the joy of the following situations?

- Where before all we knew how to do was run and hide, recovery-love reaches out to us, saying: "It's okay. You are okay. You can be just who you are here."
- Where before our whole lives were spent standing out in the dark looking in at the party of life, recovery-love reaches out to us, saying: "It's okay. Come. Take my hand. We will go in together."
- Where before all we knew how to do was control and manipulate, recovery-love reaches out to us, saying: "It's okay. Let go. You don't need to carry the weight of the world anymore."
- Where before all we knew how to do was hit and bully, recovery-love reaches out to us, saying: "It's okay. We know you were hurt. You don't need to hurt others to be loved."

- Where before all we knew how to do was be miserable and afraid, recovery-love reaches out to us, saying: "It's okay. Joy works. Laughter is welcome here. We won't steal your happiness."
- Where before all we knew how to do was work, be busy, and produce, recovery-love reaches out to us, saying: "It's okay. You are more than what you do. We love and accept you, not just what you can do. Sit down. Let me carry the water for a while."

A thousand more examples could be given, but they aren't necessary. You get the point—reality is optional once we see the difference. It is then that we have a choice. Sometimes this choice takes the courage of a warrior and the humility of a saint. So what? That is the price of gaining the promises of the Big Book. Whatever else recovery might be, it demands the making of these daily decisions. Recovery for life is all about taking a new path. That new path is always about love. On the deepest, most profound level of our being, or anyone else's being, recovery is going home.

Recovery does not necessarily mean that the old lies leave for good. It means that we learn to live a new life, crooked timber and all, in a new present, by the decisions we make. The enemy may remain. The point is that those old lies are no longer in control of who we are and how we act or what we contribute to the future.

Once we recognize the inappropriate, exaggerated, or just plain crazy impulses we use to respond to events that trigger us in the present time (by whatever label you want to use), isn't recovery for us a matter of choosing not to go there? Isn't recovery then the willingness to intercept the "flawed thinking" the Big Book talks about and reframe whatever is going on around us according to our new truths, based on the self-compassion and self-confidence we learn in the fellowship?

Isn't that what all the meetings, readings, meditation, prayer, and service work are about? Isn't that what all those recovery behaviors do? They give us the inspiration, motivation, and example to make the decisions to do the next right thing, even if that next right thing involves swimming upstream against lifelong, practiced habits.

CHILDREN OF THE LIGHT

Swimming upstream is tough work. Thank God none of us have to do it alone. There are always those in recovery ahead of us, children of the light, who will lend a hand and show us the way forward. The God of our understanding reaches out through people, through the fellowship, to lift up what has fallen flat and to heal what has been broken.

Yes, we have been beaten and battered, and we have done a good job of knocking ourselves silly. We have done harm to others; we have repeatedly fallen into the holes we have sworn again and again that we would avoid. And we have gotten up. We have tried again. And along the way we have reached out to help anyone we could to climb up the mountain with us. However dark the evil tide may be that swirls around us, there is also light. The light is always there. We need never be victims, no matter what trouble has found its way to our door.

Think of the miracles of lives found and hearts healed in your group. Then multiply that by the number of groups, meetings with sponsors, and countless acts of service taking place all over this world. If the miracle happens in your group, then it happens in others as well. Miracles enable the members of our recovering families to stand in that tide and say, "No more." Here it ends.

QUESTIONS

1. What is the "evil tide" of history in your recovery story?
2. Why is it important to recognize your "old lie" in your recovery efforts?
3. Why is it important to establish your "new truth" in your recovery efforts?

MOVING ON TO CHAPTER 8

But for some, the journey of recovery takes another dip after Stage II Recovery. For some, there is another dark and dangerous place full of fears and shadows to negotiate through. Not for all, but for some.

Stage III Recovery:
The Legacy of Childhood Abuse
in Recovery

Some people in recovery are survivors of childhood abuse.
While everyone in recovery has a sad story to tell, not everyone
has experienced the damage done by childhood abuse. If this
legacy of childhood abuse is present in our adult life, it must be
addressed if full recovery is to be achieved. This level of life work
is called Stage III Recovery.

Once more the redline on our map of recovery to joy and
abundance moves on. For some of us, this line moves into a
darker and more terrifying area than we ever imagined. In part,
that is why we never imagined or faced it before.

HERE BE MONSTERS

Ancient mapmakers simply wrote "here be monsters" over the
entire area that existed beyond their knowledge and experience. Human beings have always been terrified of the unknown,
especially if they sense monsters lurking there. Everyone in recovery has Stage II Recovery or life work to do if they are to
move toward their final destination of abundance and joy. En
route to this final destination they are sure to cross a few areas
where "here be monsters." But for some, the monsters are
scarier. For those dealing with the legacy of childhood abuse,

these monsters are like a birthmark—they are always there. For example, everyone at times feels lost. For some, however, the sense of loss feels permanent. Everyone at times feels vulnerable and overwhelmed. Some, however, feel relentlessly pursued by a nameless danger that cannot be outrun or defeated. Everyone at times gets angry and feels the load they are asked to carry is too heavy. Some, however, aren't able to shake the feeling of being hounded and bludgeoned by a gigantic injustice they can neither fight nor avoid. The list could go on and on.

THE CARDS WE'RE DEALT

No damage to the human spirit need be permanent. We are all human beings and are called to live the best life we can with the cards we are dealt. The hunger for intimacy is the deepest need of a human being. All damage not dealt with becomes an obstacle to intimacy. Recovery is reclaiming the ability to dip our cup into that well of intimacy. The deeper the hurt, the longer the reach down that well. Stage III Recovery is for those of us who have to reach a long, long way down that well. Why do we have to reach so far? The answer is effects of abuse, especially childhood abuse.

The human spirit has incredible resilience. Healing can happen no matter how deep the damage. That healing may be different from anything we could have imagined, but it happens. Others have done it, and so can we. But first we must be honest, open, and willing to undertake a "searching and fearless" look at who we are, where we want to go, and the nature of what is holding us back. For those who experienced childhood abuse, there is an additional step we must take before we will be able to experience the "happy, joyous, and free" life. We can't achieve freedom or joy when we are constantly at war with the unrecognized and poorly understood monsters in our heads. We cannot defeat or outrun what we don't understand.

You've heard statements like these: "It was wrong for my father to sexually abuse me, but that was a long time ago, and I never think about it anymore," or "I hated it when my father (or mother) got drunk and got into such terrible fights. I hid in my bed and pretended I was someone else. But they don't drink anymore, so it is like it never happened," or "My father didn't mean to knock me out all those times," or "Things weren't tough at home; it was just that no one was ever there," or "When I was five, my mom beat me so badly with an iron pole they thought I might die. But I love her and will never talk about such things again," or "I'll never forget being locked up in the closet for being bad. It was terrible, but I now understand my mother was sick. She couldn't help herself." The stories go on and on.

Adults "not knowing better" or "not being able to help it" or "doing the best they can" in no way diminishes the effects of abuse on children. Loving those adults does not preclude honestly facing the truth of what happened. Denial blocks a person from embracing reality. Without reality, there is no genuine acceptance. And without genuine acceptance, there can be no real forgiveness, love, or loyalty.

It doesn't matter whether those adults from our past have recovered, changed, or even died. The harm that was done to us at the time still travels with us. It's the legacy of abuse—the area covered by Stage III Recovery. It doesn't matter why they did it. It is now our responsibility to bind up the wounds, hammer out the dents, and chase the ghosts from our haunted house. Our recovery has nothing to do with "them" or why they did or didn't do whatever brought harm to our door. For our recovery here and now, we and we alone are responsible.

BETRAYED INNOCENCE

It is a risk bringing up topics like abuse in a book for and about Twelve Step recovery. I know that. Many of our number want to hear nothing about slippery, messy, difficult issues such as the effects of childhood abuse on recovery. But it is there. The issue doesn't disappear because it is messy and difficult. I don't know how else to be loyal to the "searching and fearless moral inventory" but have it extend to "all our affairs." If we are truly honest with ourselves and find the need to pursue Stage III Recovery because of childhood abuse, then that is the road that we must follow. We will see how the early betrayal of innocence does indeed affect "all our affairs."

You know the stories. They come from our own lives or the life stories that surround us. You've heard countless tales just like these:

- Nan, a little girl whom her brother and his friends "played with" while she floated up to the ceiling, where no one could touch her. Today, nearly forty years later, she has no idea why she is apparently incapable of maintaining a relationship. She thinks she's going crazy. She must learn to connect the dots.

- Dean, who, as a child, was left with an alcoholic grandfather who chased the boy around the farm, shooting bullets over his head. Today, decades later, he has no idea why he can't even watch an intense movie at the theater without thinking that the old lady walking past him has a gun hidden in her popcorn box. He thinks he's going crazy. He must learn to connect the dots.

- Danny, who seemed willing to die rather than face or even admit any of this "abuse nonsense." He discloses that all that happened to him was just that his brother blew his brains out while standing next

to him when he was two years old. He admits no
abuse, but he does think he is going crazy. He must
learn to connect the dots.

And the angels wept and still weep at the horror of this
childhood abuse brought forth into present-day life. How will
this cycle of disaster ever be broken if we do not face and bring
light into this place of such terrible darkness? And how can we
do this if we do not understand and recognize this legacy of
abuse where it exits in our adult lives?

THE SYMPTOMS OF ABUSE

I know from experience the resistance a person can feel at even
the mention of the word *abuse*. This resistance comes from
many places, not the least of which is a faulty understanding
of loyalty to those in our past. Loyalty and love do not preclude
telling and facing the truth.

I have found it a mistake to look only at the experiences of
our past to judge the presence or absence of abuse. Look rather
at the *symptoms* of abuse in our present lives. If the symptom is
there, then the cause has to have been there as well. It is a mystery why some people with horrible stories seem relatively un-
touched by the abuse (meaning their lives show few of the
symptoms of the early abuse), while the symptoms in the following discussion are in full bloom in the lives of others with
seemingly mild stories. The story isn't the point so much as
what we took away from the early experiences. And if what we
took away is at the bottom of these symptoms, then this whole
process of childhood abuse leading to the adult acting out of
the symptoms must be faced and dealt with if we are to gain
abundance and joy as human beings. After the early abuse has
stopped, the legacy remains. And that legacy is as much a part
of us as are our fingerprints.

TAKE THE EARLY ABUSE TEST

See if you relate to any of the following symptoms of abuse. You may find it helpful to rate yourself on a scale of 1 to 10 after each symptom described. Placing a 10 after the symptom means you can totally relate, while the number 1 means you cannot relate at all.

DISASSOCIATION: This is like living your life inside a room made of bulletproof glass. Life just seems to go by. Long ago, you learned it wasn't safe to be "here" in your body, so you left. Nobody else knows that you "aren't there." This bulletproof glass room allows you to see what is happening around you while protecting you from the danger that you know is out there. You cannot move forward in your program by making the critical connections we have spoken of when you "aren't there" to be in a relationship in the first place. It's impossible to have a relationship with someone who isn't there. Disassociation prevents relationship from forming with God, self, and others. Those of us in need of Stage III work can talk the program, yet we know we have a deeper level to us that is full of broken glass. So we just never go to this hidden, detached aspect of our lives. Maybe it's because we don't know where "there" is. Maybe it's because it just scares us too much. But the God of our understanding cannot heal what we will not own. The only thing worse than facing the fears that exist on this level is what happens to us if we don't. Failure to take the power of our program to this level means that the tragedy of the past wins, not only in our lives, but in the lives of those we allow this evil to pass to.

How do you relate to disassociation?
Rate yourself on a scale of 1 to 10 _____

PSYCHIC NUMBING: Psychic numbing is about the disconnect with feelings that abuse causes. We learn it isn't safe to feel, and so we just unplug at an early age. Later in recovery, we find it is not easy to find that outlet to plug back into. How many times have we envied people in touch with their feelings, people who can celebrate, have fun, get excited about something? Yet we have no idea what those emotions would feel like. How many times have we pretended to feel a certain way because it was expected or appropriate, but we knew it was only part of our act? How many times have we wished for and maybe prayed that we could or would feel something special at an important event in our lives—such as a graduation or even the birth of a child or grandchild—but the best we could generate was, at most, a small emotional spark? It's like a firefly lighting up in total darkness for the briefest of seconds, then nothing but darkness. It's not that the feelings don't exist. It's that we do not have access to them. How often have you felt cut off from your feelings?

How do you relate to psychic numbing?
Rate yourself on a scale of 1 to 10 _____

EXAGGERATED RESPONSES: Everything is extreme to an abuse survivor. Our emotional response is blown hugely out of proportion because it is seen and felt through the eyes and nervous system of the child whose life was in mortal danger. We always feel we are in danger and have no idea what being safe would feel like. Because we don't know what being safe is, we don't know what danger is, either. So, we often put ourselves in harm's way without seeing the danger till the hammer falls. How often have we "killed a mosquito with a shotgun"? How often have we experienced an overwhelming emotional response to something minor?

How do you relate to exaggerated responses?
Rate yourself on a scale of 1 to 10 _____

HYPERVIGILANCE: This is about always being on guard. It is about panic at being caught in a crowd. Any crowd. Even maybe a crowd of mall Christmas shoppers. We experience extreme discomfort anytime we can't have our back against the farthest wall so we can view the entire room. How often have we felt in danger when we weren't? How often have we reacted to an everyday situation as if we were in the middle of a war? And how often did we later feel terribly ashamed about that reaction?

How do you relate to hypervigilance?
Rate yourself on a scale of 1 to 10 _____

EASILY OVERWHELMED: When we are overwhelmed, our hearts often pound loudly and our pulse races. We often feel the need to find a place to hide. Being overwhelmed is when having five things to get at the grocery store seems too much. When a list of three "to-dos" makes us feel like we will never get it all done. When planning a trip that requires three stops makes it too complicated to even start. When being forced to wait in line, we are overwhelmed with the feeling that someone is doing damage to us on purpose. Being easily overwhelmed has to do with our nervous systems being impaired and ordinary tasks—at least ordinary for most people—becoming too much to even think about.

How do you relate to being easily overwhelmed?
Rate yourself on a scale of 1 to 10 _____

THE NEXT STEP

Again, I'm not a doctor. My short list of symptoms or your rating of them is not a diagnosis. But, if our goal in recovery as human beings is to experience eventual abundance and joy, then a score of 5 or above under any symptom is a reason for concern and may best be handled by seeking out a health care professional who specializes in trauma cases. I do not pretend to offer anything like a comprehensive treatment for this emergence from repression of childhood abuse. My goal is to raise a flag. It is to legitimize this most painful and dangerous time necessary in our recovery for those for whom it fits.

Let this small test raise a red flag that says, "Abuse counts." Anyone who relates to the thoughts offered in this chapter has an absolute right to address his or her pain. Recovery must allow for dealing with this pain if we are to be faithful to the intention and spirit of the program.

I realize that everyone's recovery path is not the same. Many of us will not relate to these symptoms, or to the depth I am describing here. But just because this level of recovery may not be part of our recovery experience does not mean that it is not part of another's recovery path.

It's time this legacy of abuse (Stage III Recovery) comes out of the closet. It's time we come to understand we are first of all human beings in recovery. It is time to understand the effect of Stage III Recovery on our efforts to lead spiritual lives. Who we are says nothing about who God is. But it says everything about who God is to us. The unrecognized and untreated forces of abuse have profound influence on who we are.

WHEN THE EGG BREAKS

Not all trauma includes repression. For example, an adult who witnesses a fatal car accident may have trauma in his or her life, but it is not necessarily repressed. Childhood abuse is different. There is almost always deep, violent, powerful repression with childhood abuse. For a host of reasons, there's an urgent need to push the pain, confusion, sadness, and rage as far beneath consciousness as possible. We scream, "It cannot be true; therefore it does not exist!" The greater the degree of betrayal and the length of time we push it away from us, the more powerful it becomes.

Once we are in recovery, we stop medicating our feelings. We begin to face our fear of where honesty would lead us. We risk reaching out. We begin to scrape away the rock at the core of our souls. We tentatively begin to open doors. Some of us have no idea at the start of Stage III Recovery how powerful the repressed forces are behind our locked doors. At some point, for some of us, all that has been repressed begins to surface. What comes out is neither healthy nor happy. The emotions are so powerful that a rough kind of violent, bitter insanity often follows. We suddenly realize our emotional life was arrested at a point where repression became our way of life. In fact, our maturity was stopped there. Maturity is the healthy separation from others so we become able to stand on our own values, as individuals, as adults, and make our decisions from that independent position. Repression eliminates that healthy separation. If not brought into recovery, the legacy of abuse forever fixates a person at the age and in the circumstance in which the repression began. This repression and the pain that causes it are the headwaters of the evil tide. Imagine yourself as an egg, and then imagine it breaking open. This is how this powerful and profound emergence of self from repression feels. Repression damages our capacity for a healthy relationship that brings us love, safety, and a sense of belonging. This increased awareness that comes with Stage III Recovery enlarges our hunger for the love we never had rather than diminishes the need. In turn, our desire for love grows while our ability to function in healthy relationships withers. And so comes the torment. Once more, I do not pretend to offer anything like a comprehensive treatment of this emergence from repression. My goal is to legitimize this most painful and dangerous place in the life of people recovering from childhood abuse. They need to know that this time of such upheaval will not last forever. No matter how upended and desperate we may feel today while this emergence from repression takes place, it is all part of our recovery journey.

If we take this time now and do the work, the road will level out. Emotions will cool. We will feel and be less vulnerable. What will emerge is a better, happier, and healthier human being than we ever thought possible. And as the spirituality of the program teaches us, we may even eventually give thanks for this terrible passage. Why? Because it has given us the power to touch people who are in this agonizing place when others cannot reach them because they've never been there. If we've been there, we know. And God can and will best use our worst times to reach out to those still suffering.

WE WALK A CROOKED ROAD

Those of us who were not taught life's first critical lessons of love and belonging walk funny through life. We wobble. Our way is not as others'. We start from a very different place. We see different images when we close our eyes and hear very different sounds in our heads when something slips through our tightly controlled gateway. We need to learn to stop beating ourselves up and figure out how to get a better pair of glasses that provides a different vision, one that does not start from the tormented soul of a child. No matter what obstacles and monsters stand in our way, we must go as deep as the hurt. Hurt people limp. But we can learn that limping isn't so bad, especially if we are walking with others who limp as we do. If we learn to lean on each other, none of us limp as badly. It doesn't matter whether we go forward with a sprint or a limp, just as long as we move forward. We also belong at the banquet table of recovery.

QUESTIONS

1. If there was abuse in your childhood, how has it affected your adult recovery?
2. Why is it so difficult for survivors of childhood abuse to admit that abuse is part of their story?
3. What symptom of abuse do you most closely relate to?

MOVING ON TO CHAPTER 9

The harder the work, the more important it is to keep our eye on the goal: abundance and joy. So what is there to be said about abundance and joy? Read on.

CHAPTER 9

Abundance and Joy:
The Goal of Recovery

❦

Abundance and joy is the goal of recovery. Abundance is experienced differently by different people. None of us can judge what abundance is or should be for another person or how much joy he or she should experience since we have no way of knowing what the conversation is like between someone else and the God of his or her understanding.

Once more the redline running through the heart of our lives on our map of recovery moves on. It moves in response to the call emerging from the deepest part of our souls, a call we now hear more clearly as we travel further into our story, creating newer and better consequences by the decisions we are now able to make.

THIS PLACE OF ABUNDANCE AND JOY

This call to move on, to go deeper, like everything in recovery, is woven from mystery and soaked in wonder. We must keep moving. In truth, there is no such thing as "finally arriving" at joy and abundance. Joy and abundance is not a place. It is a journey, an attitude, a state of being. Yes, moving into the "state of joy and abundance" is our destination, but this state of grace is different for everyone—there's no "one size fits all," and the journey is everlasting. *Abundance* is the term we use here to describe moving deeper into God as we move deeper into ourselves. As our experience of God deepens day by day, year after year, we increasingly move from self-reliance to God-reliance. There is no one face of joy and abundance. Who we are called to be is far too grand for that. Just think of the faces we've seen moving through the stages of recovery as we lengthen our stride in our journey upward, inward, and onward.

Where have we seen the face of abundance in our recovery? What did it look like? What message did it carry for us?

ONE FACE OF ABUNDANCE

Halfway through a presentation I was giving at an addictions conference in the Deep South, a back door opened and in came a dozen or so new attendees. I could feel their vibrations all the way to the front. As my mouth carried on just fine, my mind said, "The folks from corrections have arrived."

There was one person shepherding this rough-looking group. Ms. Phyllis was in her late sixties, plump, maybe five feet tall, and certainly not in top physical condition. If any in her group wanted to run, she wouldn't have been able to chase them down. If they wanted to get physical, she couldn't defend herself. But it was obvious Ms. Phyllis was in complete charge. Sometimes in overwhelming abundance, the spirituality of the program settles in a person creating superior power. It was so with Ms. Phyllis.

After the presentation, I found Ms. Phyllis in a rather crowded, narrow hallway behind our conference room. I wanted to talk with her. Ms. Phyllis acknowledged that she was with a court-ordered treatment center. So crowded were the prisons in the state that if a felony was committed by persons under the influence of alcohol or other drugs, they often were sent to her facility first rather than prison.

Down this narrow hallway came one of her charges. Donald

stood maybe six foot four and looked like he was made of bowling balls. He had the convict strut and the stare to go with it. As Donald strutted down the hallway, others pressed themselves against the walls to let him pass. You'd have to be blind not to know it wasn't a good idea to get in his way. As he walked toward us, Ms. Phyllis moved in front of him, reached up, and patted his face. "This is Donald," she continued. "He's my baby. Donald's a fine man. Donald is going to make it."

I asked him what he thought of Ms. Phyllis. In a voice that rolled like thunder, he said, "I love her." When asked if he was going to make it, he said, "I'll make it or die trying." As he marched off, I said to Ms. Phyllis something about not wanting to ever get sideways of Donald. She said, "Yes, he murdered a man with his bare hands in a drug deal gone bad. But really, underneath he is a pussycat."

There aren't enough guns, clubs, prisons, or solitary confinement cells in the world to break men like Donald. The more you beat them, the stronger they get. They know all about violence, but they are strangers to love. They know all about danger and betrayal. It's safety and trust they've never experienced. Not until someone like Ms. Phyllis comes along. Love, real love, recovery-love is the only thing stronger than whatever in us is hurt or damaged.

ABUNDANCE IS . . .

Recovery-love isn't about theory. *It's about what works and only what works.* Only love offered by a truly spiritual person can pat the face of a murderer and say, "This is my baby; he's a good man." Only such love accepted enables that same man to say, "I'll make it or I'll die trying." How would you describe abundance? Maybe something like this:

Abundance is what we discover as we allow the hand that is God to fill the glove that we are.

Abundance is God's fingerprint unmistakably imprinting and changing us as we follow the Red Road.

Abundance is raising our hearts and hands to God though we are broken and our path is still filled with broken glass and rusty nails.

Abundance is the choice to let go even though we are scared to death, trusting God will catch us.

Abundance is acting in favor of the absolute certainty of the righteousness of a life surrendered to God, even when that certainty doesn't feel all that certain.

Abundance is the reward of coming to regard ourselves with as much love as others in the fellowship regard us with, no matter how misplaced or undeserved we feel their love toward us may be.

Abundance is allowing ourselves to learn by experience, deep in our beings, that the greatest gift indeed is in receiving the recovery-love offered us and not merely in giving it. Giving without receiving breaks the wheel in half.

Abundance is about hearing and obeying the Voice of God within, even when it tells us to go where we would much rather not.

Abundance is not about how much of the spotlight I get, but about how many others I have been willing to help find their own light.

Abundance is not about ego as exalting self, but as a willingness to do our work and confront our inner ghosts so that we may be of better service to our God. This healing helps us to arrive at a deeper knowledge of self so that whatever and however terrible the defects we hold up to grace to be healed are, we can, by that healing, then be of greater service in reaching out to others.

Abundance is all about spirituality. Spirituality is all about openness to the Voice of God. The Voice of God is always about the call to move further into recovery and spiritual life.

HERE COMES THE BIG DOG

Neil lovingly calls God "the Big Dog." He also uses that term for anyone he finds God in. Neil recently told me of a kind of meditation he and other Twelve Steppers did on a retreat that I thought spoke well of abundance. The retreat leader took them to four places. First, he told them to imagine that they were in a big-time basketball game. It was vitally important that they win. The problem was that the other team was much better than they were. They were bigger, stronger, faster, and could all jump like kangaroos. During a time-out, their losing team huddled together, more in misery than anything else. They knew they couldn't win, no matter how important it was that they do so. The opposing team was just too powerful. As they look up, Michael Jordan comes striding out of the locker room. And he is wearing their jersey. As Neil put it, "The Big Dog himself has shown up."

The group was then led in meditation to a very different place—an alley. The leader explained that they were getting beat up by men stronger and tougher than they were. Suddenly, through a haze of blood and pain, a shadow comes down the alley. It's Muhammad Ali in his prime. The great fighter pulls off the tormentors. He stands over the participants and tells the men beating them up that if they want to continue the beating, they have to come through him.

The leader of the retreat took the men to a third place. They were told to imagine that they were flat broke and it was their son's birthday. They wanted to get their son a great present so badly they could taste it. They were standing in front of the big display window of a huge sports store, where they could see just the present they wanted to get. The problem was they were flat broke. Out of nowhere a man walks up and stands next to them. They start talking, and the participants explain the bind they are in. The stranger then tells them, "Well, my name is

John D. Rockefeller, and I own the store. You come in with me, and you can have any damn thing you want."

Finally, the leader directed them to a church. It was the funeral of a friend they knew who was mighty in the way of the spirit but never raised much of a blip on the radar screen of normal life. But they knew the value and grandeur of his life. Few people attended this funeral. The church was almost empty. The person hired to sing not only wasn't much of a talent, but also seemed bored to tears. Just then a mighty and glorious sound begins to fill the church like golden light. The participants spin around, looking up to the choir loft, and there stands Mahalia Jackson with a full choir in splendid robes. She says she is singing for this great person as he passes to the fulfillment of the promise.

After each meditation, the leader asks how it feels to be rescued from a hopeless, helpless situation. Everyone thought it felt pretty darn good. The retreat leader then told them they always had access to power greater even than Michael Jordan, Muhammad Ali, John D. Rockefeller, or Mahalia Jackson combined. And all they had to do was just ask, open that door, and take the gift that has already been given. We are not alone in our walk. The Big Dog will show up for us. There is no such thing as being powerless when we take our seat in God's pocket. Abundance is knowing we have access to that privileged place.

FAITH IS PART OF THE EQUATION

Spiritual abundance has nothing to do with financial or physical abundance. There is no equating of abundance with dollars when we are in the Twelve Step fellowship. We are surrounded by examples of spiritual abundance in lives that were anything but financially successful. Abundance is what happens to us when we learn to let go. It involves surrendering, which is not only an act of faith, but also of trust. Faith is easy. It is trust that is hard. Especially when so many of us have been so sorely damaged exactly at that point of learning to trust. I have always found deep meaning in the saying "Faith takes us to the fortieth-floor window. Trust jumps."

Those in the Twelve Step fellowship have experienced the transforming power of jumping out that high window. Abundance is going for it, taking that next frightening step forward. It's risking the move into the next level of recovery. Something incredibly grand is achieved by becoming willing to take that leap, to surrender that "one last thing" we hang on to so desperately in the false assumption that we need it.

The bird never knows it can fly until it jumps from the safety of the nest. Only when it does can that bird know that it will never again need to seek safety by hiding in that now-empty nest. Just like this bird, we cannot barricade ourselves in a cave of comfort that we've created. Safety isn't about hiding. Instead, it's about gathering strength, skills, and support, knowing that we can handle anything that comes down the road at us. We learn by experience that not only can we cope, but we can thrive. That's because we are not alone. We have resources. We are surrounded by giants. As unimaginable as it once seemed, we come to the realization that we belong and we are special.

For the wounded who are still fixated at a point of pain in their lives, it takes time to jump. We do it in stages. Sometimes we are prodded by terrible inner and outer pain. As we struggle at that point of our arrested growth, more often than not, when it is time, an angel shows up. It's often human angels who cross our paths at "just the right time" to escort us onward. At first, unaccustomed to the light, we deflect their offers like a flat stone bounced over the surface of a lake. We are like children counting the bounces as the stone sails away. Unlike children in a game, though, we deeply and sometimes desperately hope that stone comes back to us.

We so want to see what is over the next hill after living so long in the valley. These angels sent to us say: "I'll go with you. We will go together because I want to see over that hill as well. We will hold hands and go up that road trusting that what we find is infinitely better than what we left behind. We will go together and in that fellowship break each other's chains."

Oh how our hearts yearn to jump, to fly.

We are afraid. Yet inch by inch, moved both by the pain of not jumping and by the faithful, loving hand holding ours, we move to the edge of the nest. We know we sense our souls are being called to fly. The God of recovery-love calls us to rise up from the dead. When it is time, our inner voice tells us, "Jump! Be done with fear and chains."

LOVE WAS THERE ALL ALONG

It is no small thing to be loved. Love has no dark corners, no secrets. When we finally surrender, we discover something amazing. We discover that love was there all the time. Only our fear and our inability to connect the dots kept us from seeing it.

The more deeply denied the love, the more difficult it will be for people to learn that they are acceptable, they count, and they are good enough. I'm not talking about the kind of difficulty that we associate with learning to play the piano. Learning to play the piano may take a lot of time and practice, but no monsters are hiding in the keyboard. No evil tide lurks there. But monsters of all sorts live at the exact spot where we would participate in the miracle of recovery-love. And it is to this exact spot that recovery and the God of our understanding comes like a heat-seeking missile. It's not because God likes to see us struggle. It's because that's where we are fixated. That is where our passage to joy and abundance is blocked. That is the bottleneck through which the river of recovery must pass. And so here is where our faithful God of recovery comes because here is where our freedom must be won.

Have you noticed, maybe in retrospect, that no matter how much we fought the pull of recovery-love and deflected any bit of it, divine and human, it just keeps coming on like the sun and rain falling on hard ground? Recovery-love doesn't quit because God never quits calling us to abundance and joy. Can you relate to this pull of recovery-love and our pushing it away? When we hide, it keeps seeking us out. When we say, "No, no," recovery-love keeps saying, "Yes, yes."

Recovery is hearing the call that asks us to step forward when we are nestled in the safety of the anonymity of a crowd. It's accepting that we are chosen, that we are the ones, that we are special, that we are loved. Abundance is bravely accepting that call regardless of our hesitation, doubts, and horrendous fear of vulnerability. Healing is the result. The program tells us to carry this message to others who can't accept their own worth and beauty. We tell others to let us love them until they are able to love themselves. And there it is, to whatever degree we are able to embrace it and claim it and grab it and crawl up into its lap—there is abundance and joy.

HOW GRAND IS GRAND?

Can a "drunk" ever do or be anything grand? Can ongoing recovery ever be called grand? It really depends on what we think grand is all about. What makes grand, grand? How grand is recovery? Ours or anyone else's? How grand is it to see the absolutely dead and gone get up and walk again? And maybe even learn to dance?

I for one do not believe there is anything grander or more important in all the swirl of human existence than recovery. What could possibly be more important than a human being coming back from the dead? Others may scoff at the terminology "coming back from the dead." But we know, we experience, in a way others never will, that that is exactly what recovery is. Only when a person has been in the deepest darkness can he or she fully appreciate the glory of the light.

If we want abundance and joy, we must go where it is. We must pay attention. We must listen and watch. It doesn't matter how scary the concept of abundance and joy sounds to us. If we would reap the reward, we must be willing to pay the price. Going halfway doesn't get the job done.

Can you relate to this? If so, repeat the following often.

I would know the joy of Abundance.
My voice said, know first of God.
I would know of God.
My voice said, know first of faith.
I would know of faith.
My voice said, know first of trust.
I would know of trust.
My voice said, know first of self.
I would know of self.
My voice said, know first of silence.
I would know of silence.
My voice said, I am afraid.
A deeper voice still said,
Good, you have begun.

QUESTIONS

1. How would you define *abundance*?
2. Why is the concept of abundance important in understanding your recovery?
3. What are three examples of abundance in your life of recovery today?

MOVING ON TO CHAPTER 10

It's all so basic. Recovery is about basics. Recovery as a human adventure is all about getting back to basics. A map of recovery is a map of the basics. But what basics might those be?

Getting Back to Basics

Some Things Never Change: The Truth Is Forever

~

There are basics for an honest, effective program. Those basics are expressed first as attitudes. Behaviors then carry those attitudes into lived life. Attitudes are expressions of the spiritual principles our program is founded on.

The map to abundance and joy has always existed. It has always been about the basics. Sometimes we just forget what those basics are.

WHERE'S YOUR DOGS?

Recently, I talked with a priest, Father Bill, who blessed me when we parted. I felt truly blessed. He is over seventy years old and is in charge of the adolescent program at a large treatment center. It's hard to imagine anyone that age with the energy and flexibility to connect with youth. But obviously "youth" is the stage he was picked to dance on—and what a dance he does. It's all love, of course. Recovery always is about love.

Bill says, "The more troubled the kid is, the more I like 'em." His face nearly glowed as he spoke of "his guys and gals." He also serves a parish near the treatment center. After feeling loved and accepted by the priest, many of the youth who leave the center come to his Sunday services each week. Every liturgy begins with Bill shouting to the congregation, "Hey, you guys." They answer back from the same deep level where Father Bill has connected with them, "Hey you, Father." For many, he is the first safe father they have ever known. Almost sheepishly, Bill said his kids taught him the meaning of the phrase "Where's your dogs?" "It's some kind of rap thing," he says. It means, "Who has your back? Who protects you?"

After his rather unusual greeting at Mass, he then asks, "Where's my dogs?" You never have to worry who's got your back when you lead with love. All his once-lost children answer in their own language by barking and snarling. Translation: "We are right here, Father."

Back to basics. When you meet the really real, they shine like neon at midnight.

THE JOURNEY OF TRANSFORMATION STARTS WITH THE BASICS

The basics of recovery, at any stage, are about honesty. They are about learning to honor ourselves and others by getting straight about rights—rights claimed and rights given. They are about the willingness to be led and the bravery, one hand in God's and one in our peers', to go where the road leads no matter how frightening the journey. We are all told this journey of transformation happens by observing basics like going to meetings, having a sponsor, connecting with a Higher Power, doing service work, and reading recovery literature like the Big Book. In my experience, behaviors are always what is talked about when the subject is getting back to basics.

But actions can lie, just like words can. Meetings can land in a comfort zone where everyone is perfectly content to just sit around saying the same old things with very little self-revelation and therefore very little growth taking place. "Having a sponsor" can become some pale, vague notion of when there's trouble, there's someone to call. Surely having a sponsor means a great deal more than this. Some people read recovery literature not as a means to become more spiritual but to collect ammunition to defend their set notions of what is or is not "program."

Attitude and Spirit Count

Behavior alone is not the bottom line of getting back to basics. The attitude or spirit behind the behaviors is what carries the big stick. Attitudes are the first and real meaning of what it means to get back to basics. The basics are not merely about compliance to a prescribed form of behavior. They are about the spirit of commitment and generosity that gives the behavior power and meaning.

Father Bill could view his spending time with these damaged, addicted kids as a punishment. But he does not. Getting back to real basics translates to Father Bill beginning his Mass overwhelmed by the goodness and beauty he sees in his charges before him. He sees gold where nearly everyone else only saw trouble.

The teens are overwhelmed by the magic of this good man before them, who has done so much to lead them out of the wilderness. This man, who was not afraid of their pain or their journey, magically passed through their facade of deflected love as easily as an eagle passes through mist. As did Ms. Phyllis with her felons or Jimmy R., who was old and sick but still went into the bitter cold to his Friday meeting because "Maybe I can be of help to someone else." You know such great-souled people. Their power, the basics, is not in what they do but in who they are.

Only the true basics that, first of all, come from a person's spirit allows for this kind of spiritual power. If you hear the music, then you recognize the dance. The dance of recovery is always about finding, then following, then becoming more of a person who makes a difference, first of all in ourselves, then for as many as we are able to help up the mountain.

Six Basic Recovery Attitudes

I'd like to suggest six basic attitudes we refer to in recovery all the time. They are as familiar to us as our breakfast cereal, but you'll more often than not go hungry looking for them in the "normal world." This list is best understood not in a linear fashion. Instead, it should be viewed as a circle where nothing has a

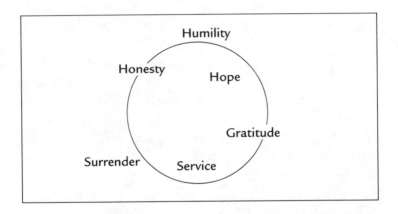

definite start or ending, with one attitude blending into another.

1. *Honesty*

It's not just about telling the truth. That, of course, is a kind of honesty, but I'm referring to the basic stance a person in recovery takes toward his or her life. I'm talking about depth. I'm talking about the opening up of our whole lives to the power of recovery as it happens in "all our affairs." I'm talking about the kind of life we are led into when we have received the miraculous gift of the First Step. For then we enter a dimension that demands we go beyond glitz, sizzle, and hype to a deeper and more real level of life. We can't be in recovery and be seduced by show. Recovery takes us by the nose and the heart and rubs our faces in what really counts in life. With this kind of honesty, there is no such thing as virtual recovery.

Honesty allows us to see and celebrate the very guts of life. We see the victory of someone showing up for group, week after week, whom others might call a bum or throw away. We celebrate every person who gets a medallion for whatever length of time in the program. Recovery takes us to the altar flame of what is real.

Honesty doesn't go into cardiac arrest over the insignificant. We learn to not sweat the small stuff, and we learn that almost everything is small stuff. But equally, we come to understand and pay attention to what is important. We have experienced that the banquet is about who is in the chairs and not what is on the table. We learn we don't need "stuff" no matter how much society screams that "stuff" is the only way to validate our worth.

As we do our best to live out the basic of honesty in our daily lives, we give witness to the importance of aspiring to the real for a truly human life. We are called to make our lives living, breathing billboards of what is important in life. Others see us. And in being seen, we give some small measure of the bread of life to the world.

2. Humility

This basic is about learning that "life isn't all about me." If recovery teaches us anything, it is this: "I am part. I am not all."

Humility allows us to rejoice in the good fortune and success of others without seeing it as a threat to our own.

Humility gets self out of the way so that there's room for others in our lives. We learn to say, "I don't always have to be talking about me!"

Humility is present when someone leaves our company feeling better about who they are, rather than feeling stuffed with facts about how great we are.

Humility is basic to that most rare skill of being able to listen. So few know how to or are able to listen. Maybe that is at least partly why there are so many lonely people haunting the world. But we try. We know that failing to listen may result in the death of a suffering brother or sister who came among us seeking a place at the table but were turned away because we didn't have room for them among us. We failed to listen to them. Others see us. And in being seen, we give some small measure of the bread of life to the world.

3. Hope

Tragically, many in our society live without hope. And as a result, they live lives full of violence, depression, and self-hatred. Life without hope truly is, as the poet Dante said, "hell."

Hope is the fingerprint of God among us and the fuel of recovery. Hope is a fundamental building block of recovery, a basic we gain as a reward when we exercise the options that working a program provides. Hope is always about options. As long as there are options, there is hope. We come to learn that no matter how hopeless the situation appears, there are options. There is another way.

Hope is the refusal to give up no matter what because there is a way out. And that way out exists because we are not alone. We have access to power beyond anything we could imagine.

Hope is the point in the Big Book where it says, "There will come a time when no power on earth will keep you sober."

There is hope shining through these bitter words because there is a power not of this earth that is ours for the asking.

Once experienced, hope becomes the motivation that refuses to let others live without hope. Since there was hope for us, there is hope for others. We give testimony to that belief by the way we live. And others see this. And in being seen, we give some small measure of the bread of life to the world.

4. Gratitude

In recovery, we either learn to be grateful, or we don't last. Gratitude is the air of recovery. Gratitude is what makes the lungs of recovery fill, the heart beat, and the life flow.

The attitude of gratitude focuses on what we have rather than what we don't. With gratitude, there is such a thing as enough. People filled with gratitude aren't good consumers because they don't heed the message "You need more stuff. Stuff will make you whole."

Gratitude makes us whole, not stuff. It allows us to make the abundant blessings we already have in our life not only count, but be enough. And not just enough, but more than we could have imagined.

Gratitude allows us to understand that there is enough for everyone so we don't have to hoard whatever it is we think we need. There is plenty.

In a culture addicted to the belief that "I need more," people with an attitude of gratitude stand out. They are like roses growing out of cracks in a ghetto neighborhood. People watch. They see. And in being seen, we give some small measure of the bread of life to the world.

5. Service

There is no recovery without service. Service is the means of paying back our debt to our Higher Power and all those who came to us in our time of desperation.

Service is not a substitute or a hiding place for us to avoid doing our own work by becoming overly busy. It is always easier to deal with someone else's "ism" than our own. Service is the opportunity we use to take the wisdom we have gained by doing our own Stage II and Stage III work back into the community.

Service works. It forces us to get out of ourselves and focus on the needs and lives of others.

Service is a statement of responsibility. Service says, "I'll do it."

Service provides the greatest of gifts. Through it, we learn that we are part of something bigger than ourselves. Anyone who would truly be of service to another has a front-row seat at the festival of miracles.

Service provides meaning that shakes off the attitude of "poor me" or "nothing ever happens around here" like a dog shakes off water. Through service, our goal is to make life better for someone else. Someone committed to service stands out. People watch. And in watching, they see. And in being seen, we give some small measure of the bread of life to the world.

6. Surrender

Many seem not to understand the nature of surrender. They see it as failure, I guess. But the surrender of our lives to a Higher Power is the greatest victory of which a human being is capable.

Surrender is not an act of weakness but rather an admission of our limitations, which then opens the door to true strength. We have learned from bitter experience that there is no one weaker than the person who has only his or her own power to rely on. Others can call the attitude of surrender anything they want, but we know the truth. In that truth is the heart of our abundance and joy.

Surrender finally allows for letting go. Only by letting go can we ever be free. We are made to move on. Our hearts are made for moving on. But fear would have us hang on and on and on. What we won't let go of will not let go of us, and it prohibits us from finding that something better that waits up ahead. We can't say hello if we don't say good-bye.

Surrender is the ultimate power trip. Once we surrender, we are able to become the conduit through which God acts in our world. There is no power greater than God. Surrender readily acknowledges that the wonders at hand aren't about us; they are about God through us. All we need to do is show up, get out of the way, and watch the show. No matter how much of "us" gets used up in the exchange, there is nothing quite so thrilling as watching God at work. Riding that lightning bolt with God is about as exciting as it gets.

As we go about our business, led onward by the basics, others watch. And in being seen, we give some small measure of the bread of life to the world.

OUR LIVES ARE A WORK IN PROGRESS

In our lives, we must learn to accept that mostly what we see is the stitches on the back of the embroidery. From the back, the work of art in progress appears a jumble of random stitches and ill-matched colors. We don't see the front of the work coming into harmony and fulfillment very often. Maybe that's it. What is asked of us is to be willing to apply our little stitches whether we see how they fit or not, trusting there is a greater hand and a greater love at work. Maybe this journey called recovery is all about the willingness to show up wherever we are sent. It doesn't matter who is watching or if anyone is ever watching. Being watched has nothing to do with it. It's the music that counts. And when we hear the music, what else is there to do but dance our hearts out the best we can?

GOD DID TIME, TOO

On a crowded, busy downtown street of a large city, Pete watched limousines roll up to a fancy auditorium. One by one, the occupants of the limos glided inside the building. They weren't movie stars or celebrities in any ordinary sense. They were gospel singers who were gathering for a gala that would be televised nationally.

Pete had seen other shows like this. They lifted his heart, made him feel good the way they sang about God and the power of redeeming lives. These singers possessed glorious voices capable of soaring emotion. They backed each other up with their extraordinary gift of music. He never doubted the sincerity of their faith or the tears that ran down their scrubbed faces and sometimes dripped down on their fashionable clothes and sequined gowns. Of course they were sincere. They obviously had a beautiful, comfortable walk with their God. Among them was not a single smudged face, torn shirt, or bloody knuckle.

Pete, too, had a comfortable walk with God, but his journey took him many places that these people had never seen. On this evening, he was on his way to a special meeting. Less than a mile from the highly illuminated auditorium, Pete went to his meeting at the Salvation Army. This place was important to him because he found sobriety there and learned to feel that maybe he was worth something. It was here that he had experienced, deep in his heart, that God had not given up on him. Tonight he was getting his two-year medallion.

When medallion time came, Big Bill, his sponsor, strolled up to the microphone like an all-pro football player being inducted into the Hall of Fame. It didn't matter that his lower teeth were missing, his hair was almost gone, and his clothes were simple. He stood there tall and proud. When Pete went up to get his medallion, we all cheered and clapped. Big Bill explained that he had met Pete in prison. They were two of the sorriest people on the face of the earth, he told us. But he said God has a special way of finding his best people at the bottom. And that is where he found them. Bill got in recovery a year earlier than Pete. He said that was so he could be there when Pete showed up. Then, with the most powerful, natural gesture, Bill took hold of his brother's hand. There they stood—two men who could eat nails with or without teeth—holding hands, basking in a light beyond any ever used on stage. Finally, Bill just looked at Pete, then at all of us. He said that God was doing time right along with both of them. And now they are doing a different kind of time together, and will be until the race is won.

The basics are what counts. The basics are what works. The basics are what we need to get back to, to whatever extent we ever strayed from them. It doesn't matter whether these basics are acted out in a church basement, mission, cathedral, or fancy high-rise. Recovery-love reaches beyond the glamour and hype, politics and popularity. Beneath the varnish is the grain. The basics are about getting to the grain.

The grain is Bill and Pete standing there holding hands and not apologizing for it one bit. The grain is understanding that, right along with everyone else cheering and celebrating Pete's two years, is God with a front-row seat. The grain is Father Bill shouting, "Where are my dogs?" And them shouting back, "Here we are. You lead; we'll follow you all the way out of hell."

QUESTIONS

1. How would you describe the basics of your program?
2. What is your connection between spiritual principles and the basics of the program?
3. Whom do you know that is a shining example of living the basics of the program?

MOVING ON TO CHAPTER 11

Fellowship is as fundamental a basic as exists in the program. None of us go well alone. None of us can do it alone. The map of recovery always leads us to the matter of fellowship. And oh my, what fabulous people we find as companions and peers along the way. What more can be said of fellowship?

CHAPTER 11

Fellowship:
With a Sling and a Stone

~

Recovery requires fellowship. The map of recovery always leads to fellowship. None of us goes well alone. The bonds of our community of fellowship transcend any relationship we have known before. Our glory is in those we travel with on our road of recovery.

Someone who had been in the fellowship for fifteen years recently said to me, "I guess I don't have to be ashamed that I am a drunk anymore." He is about as good a human being as exists on the planet. I was struck by this comment. I told him: "You aren't just 'a drunk.' You are an addict in a long and beautiful recovery. You walk with some of the greatest people who've ever lived. There is no end to the pride you should feel in your walk. You are the best that ever was." I then wrote this chapter about walking with giants with him in mind.

WALKING WITH GIANTS

I recently watched a television awards show where all the honorees were dressed in finely fitted designer fashions. The packed house cheered wildly as the winners were called to the stage. A hundred hands reached out to congratulate and acknowledge the recipients' hard-won success. This was a nationally televised event, which ensured that the recipients' achievements were all well documented. As I watched, my head couldn't help but fill with visions of other champions I have known. These brothers and sisters played on another field where wealth, fame, and recognition were no indicators of success. I know many such heroes.

We know where the real battles are fought and the real successes won. We are given the opportunity to walk with great souls in the fellowship. And the amazing part is that these heroes are anonymous. The spotlight tends to spoil authenticity like strong sunlight spoils milk.

For some things, the gods demand a meat sacrifice. Recovery requires such a sacrifice. It reverses the grief of a life headed toward disaster and transforms it into the grand journey possible once that life has been reclaimed, cleaned up, and turned around. Half measures avail nothing. If a brother in need stands in ten feet of water and those who can help are willing to go in just five feet, what good is that? As anyone who has come this way knows, all it takes is all there is.

An Impossible Victory

I've always loved the biblical story of David and Goliath because it tells the tale of another impossible victory. What insanity sends a boy to fight to the death with a seasoned warrior, and a giant, to boot? To make the point even clearer, David was sent out armed only "with a sling and a stone."

A sling and a stone? What could anyone do with a simple sling and a stone? What chance did David have? But David didn't quite go "only" with his inadequate weapons. As anyone moving through this journey of recovery knows, a sling and a stone is plenty if only we will let go and allow God to aim the stone. God never misses.

How often have we seen the "apparently insufficient" and

"not enough" kill off terrifying giants? We can, too, if only we will get out of the way. In the end, courage, practicing our principles, and surrendering to the wisdom of "I can't, God can, so I'll let him" carry the day.

There are those who think nothing of ten feet of water. Armies of them exist in the fellowship. They are simply brilliant and brilliantly simple. They seem not to see the impossibility of what they are about. They don't fear another's hell because they have faced their own. Hell can be beaten. In recovery, it is done on a daily basis.

We choose our traveling companions in life. We can choose to walk through life with someone or go it alone. We are given the option to choose the invaluable gift of going with these warriors whose scars shine like the sun. These peers reckon a sling and a stone is plenty. When I take the time to reflect on their amazing works, what I am left with is an astonished "My God! Aren't they something?"

Kate Builds Her Mighty Wall of Protection

Take Kate and her protectors, for example. Kate is a lovely, twenty-something woman who has successfully kept clean of alcohol for nearly five years now. Her downfall is heroin. Try as she might, until recently, she has suffered chronic heroin relapse. Kate wears one of the biggest tattoos I've ever seen; it covers her entire upper chest from shoulder to shoulder. It is a giant red, blue, and green butterfly. I asked her why she got such a big tattoo. She said because her butterfly symbolizes hope, and she can't live without hope. "I need it big enough so that I can't miss seeing it. I try to fly with my butterfly every day," she says with a smile.

She likes her tattoo because it is permanent. After all, nearly everyone else had given up on her. No one believed she was still trying to stop using heroin, especially her immediate family, she said. But she had been trying. Her mistake was in trying recovery alone. This time, she tried something different. This time, she surrendered to the wisdom of the program that teaches we all need a connection to others who understand us as we move along in recovery. She built a circular wall of mighty people around her with her battered, terrified soul in the middle. They understood her journey. After all, they'd been there. If all the old lies were going to seduce her this time, they had to first go through her fearsome team of protectors.

God was always one of her chosen protectors. She always believed in God, but she never accessed his power because she refused to trust anyone. By doing so, she also refused trusting God. When we push the love of others away, we also push God away. Kate began to allow others to be with her in her recovery, and God came right along with them. One of the mighty people she allowed to stand with her during tough times is John.

John had been selected from countless other gifted musicians to close a huge international AA event, where his music lifted an auditorium filled with more than 50,000 recovering people. He wasn't able to read music and had never taken a music class, yet his music had a direct feed from his soul to his fingers on the keyboard and to the words that floated from his mouth. The thirty-foot screens on either side of the stage caught the passion of his belief that flowed through his whole body: He sang of the miracle of recovery with his eyes closed, his face tilted up, and a sweet smile lightening his countenance.

A week later, he is on a different stage, this one at the Mission. Here, maybe half the keys of the piano work. But this music is far more than pitch and tone. It comes from a much deeper place. Every thirty seconds or so, Larry turns to John and shouts something like, "Tickle those ivories, John!" and off John goes on a furious lick, dead keys and all. On his face is the same sweet expression as he had when he played for the 50,000 people. Numbers don't matter. Numbers are meaningless in the realm of the spirit. In the divine economy, grandeur and success take on a whole different meaning. God is everywhere the music plays. Miracles are miracles no matter where you are.

Mary Jo is there, too. Now over seventy, she and her beloved deceased husband, George, founded the recovery arm of the Union Gospel Mission over thirty years ago. With nothing but a dream and a belief, they built a functioning monument to God made of the saved lives of this flock of God's special ones. A young drunk driver killed her only son. Mary Jo went to court to plead with the judge to show mercy to the young man who stole her son away. She spoke of the nature of the disease of alcoholism and embraced the offender in open court. Such is the depth of spirituality of this mighty woman. She stands there beside John, protecting Kate. Mary Jo doesn't walk so well anymore, and she has trouble at times seeing whom it is she is hugging and encouraging. It doesn't matter much. She figures everyone needs a hug and encouragement.

Everyone has a story to tell here. Dirk was arrested running guns into Mexico. Ask him about it now, and he'd say it wasn't a very good idea. But he was drunk then. He was always drunk then. When he was sent to prison, an old-timer told him, "The only way you are going to leave here alive, son, is if you prove to them you are crazier than they are." He did. After a few "dust-ups," he said, everything went pretty smoothly. Of course, it probably helped that Dirk is a giant. He got married not long ago. Everyone in his wedding party got a new tattoo. Dirk's is an intricate Celtic design that must be six inches wide around his massive forearm. It fits nicely there. Dirk is partial to lilacs. Something about the scent touches his soul. Maybe it is a lost memory of a happier time when he was back "home." In spring, he can even be seen walking along, a sprig of flower in his hand, softly singing and smelling the lilacs. Now all of his energy is channeled into going into the dangerous darkness where others are yet lost. He, too, has been chosen by Kate to be part of her wall of protection.

So one after another moves in next to each other. The wall is forming. Kate will have her protection. She has chosen well.

Adrian's mantra is, "I walk with Martin." Adrian is an African American and immensely proud of that. Once he was a world-class athlete, but alcohol and drugs brought that to a crashing stop. For years, he wandered through what he called "the ugliest alleys in the world." He knows the importance of someone saying, "I've got your back." In prison, someone has your back, or you don't survive. Adrian never misses his meetings. He runs a spiritual race now faster than his feet once moved down a track. He works with African American felons transitioning from prison back into the community. Not many could do this work. He does it with grace and power. It's no big deal for him to face down a 350-pound man in his group who did time for murder. "It doesn't mean nothing to me," says Adrian. "He got to get the message same as everyone else." His job, of course, pays very little. Recently he was offered a much better paying position in the corporate world. He snorted in utter contempt as he said, "Who'd work with my guys if I left?" That's Adrian. So he moves to Kate's wall. He looks her right in the eye and says, "Rest easy, little sister; I got your back. No one's going to sneak up on you again." The circle is forming.

Christie is tall, blond, and beautiful, and she has graduated magna cum laude from an Ivy League university. She is also addicted to alcohol and pills, and at one time she had an eating disorder. She is still physically addicted, of course, but she has long since walked out of the darkness of active addiction. She well knows there are not many addictions. There is only one addiction that expresses itself in many different faces. Spiritually, addiction is always about denied access to love. It is always about learning to accept love rather than deflect it. Christie is only too happy to take her place in Kate's wall. She, too, stands tall, offering Kate her love and protection. At a glance it would seem there would not be too much in common between Christie, massive Dirk, rock-solid Adrian, Mary Jo, and the others. But there is—they all hear the music. They all know the terror of the night and so understand the importance of showing up to protect a wounded soul. They all know about the map, where it goes, and why it is so important to keep on the path.

Then there is Dick, who has relapsed for the thousandth time. But he has gotten up one thousand and one times. Dick, too, takes his place. Dick seeks recovery with the intensity of a pit bull. "Faith has nothing to do with how often I fall, but only with how many times I get up," he says. There is innate nobility about a man who just won't quit, no matter how many times he gets knocked down. Then there is Denise, all five feet of her, who tells a story of use and abuse that would make anyone who listens want to protect her with all their might. Yet there she is, bright-eyed, joyful, and grateful. And more than willing to do a little protecting of her own. She's been there. She knows. She'll stand with her sister Kate as long as it takes, giving whatever it takes.

Even cancer couldn't destroy the beauty that shines from Gerri. She presently is undergoing chemotherapy, she has no hair, and her medications have puffed her up like the "dough boy," she says. But on her blue baseball hat is pinned her ten-year medallion, alongside a stitched red rose. Her strength is part of the wall, too. As is Vince's. He says he doesn't bring much to the party except he can take a punch. Vince can endure. He'll go the distance. If one of the protectors needs to take a rest or is wounded, Vince figures he can stand in for that person until he or she is able to stand strong once more. He'll be there all the way as Kate fights for freedom.

And on the inside of the circle with Kate a new God has been born. Kate's new God is safe and warm, as protective as a

Native American ceremonial blanket. She wraps it around her and knows no harm can touch her. Not now. Not anymore. Not if she chooses to stay hugged by her God and surrounded by her team, her heroes, her wall of champions.

The shadows still beckon, of course. This is still life with all its sharp edges. The shadows would pull Kate back if she allowed them. They whisper and shout to her the same old lies: "You are not good enough; you are not lovable; you are incompetent and morally defective; you are alone and always will be. No one cares about you. No one cares or ever will. Your butterfly is a lie. There is no hope. You belong to me, to the terrible horror of endless relapse, now and forever."

Where before Kate had not much choice but to be dragged down by these sharp words, she now speaks softly, yet with iron to the shadows. "If you want me, come get me," she says, "but first you have to take the sweetness from John's face. First kill him if you can; then come for me. For he has given me part and parcel of that sweetness. As it is his, so now is it mine. If you want me, steal the endless depth from Mary Jo. Take from her the shining spirituality that would tell the whole world: 'I forgive. For the life taken from me, I forgive. I forgive tragedy, horror, and the unthinkable. I send my loss into the infinite heart of my God that I may not only survive, but also become a witness to the power of forgiveness.' If you want me, first kill Mary Jo's spirit, for she has given it to me. She hugs me into her mother love. Pry me from her if you can. You tell me I am not loved or lovable, that I am defective and filled with failure. Tell that to Mary Jo. Tell her.

"If you want me, take on Dirk. Walk over him, if you can. For he now stands firm in front of me. He stands over me. His strength is my strength. He has climbed on the back of my butterfly and says, 'Little sister, let us fly to the moon.' To get me, you must go through him. If you want me, convince Adrian that I am not worth protecting. Go tell him this recovery business is a joke, that it has no meaning or consequence. Go tell him your lies that no one can climb the mountain; no one can rise above his or her station. He punches far above his weight, and he has given me his strength. He has given me the steel of this spirit forged in the darkest corner of the meanest alley in the world. You can have me only if you first beat him to the ground. I'll come with you when he no longer guards my back.

"If you want me, convince Christie that I'm too stupid to live. Go tell her that I have no one to stand for me and that I have failed in the measurement of life. Tell her I am not fashionable enough to attend the party. Christie has given me her intelligence. But more, far more, she has given me her love. She has called me family. She has taken me as kin. She, too, has moved up on the back of my butterfly, stretched out her arms to perfectly fill the shape of my wings, and said, 'Let us fly, my sister. Let hope soar.' Tell her your lies."

Kate's walls are made of the stuff of eternity. And inside and out, now, glows and pulses the fire of God, wrapped in the gentleness of a baby's touch. Her God now is both warrior king and most tender lover. He whispers to her to come to him in total trust and confidence, which shall never be betrayed. He tells Kate that he is forever faithful, forever present, and forever passionate about saving, healing, and protecting those he calls his own. And he knows his own; he recognizes them by the scars they wear and the recovery-love they pour into the world.

Such a marvelous thing, this growing awareness of the God of her understanding. Increasingly, Kate comes to see the presence of her God filling every space between, around, and in her image of her protective wall. She surrenders more and more to the enormously pleased face of this God who surrounds and fills her, who fights for her and plays unearthly beautiful music. He does this through the instruments of all the physical angels she has chosen to surround herself with. For he is composer and conductor of that music. And she knows that as long as the music plays, no harm can possibly befall her. As long as she hears the music, she shall never choose lies again. And the music is forever. God does not replace her butterfly because we all need our symbols. But her butterfly now becomes God through her tattoo. It is the same tattoo, only now its meaning has deepened, has enriched her to a degree she never imagined possible.

There is a certain kind of love affair that goes on between addicts and their drug of choice. It's a love affair that offers a seductive, deceiving, false relief of pain. Only another love affair, stronger and infinitely more authentic, is powerful enough to override that which is false. Recovery is a love affair, and Kate is now thoroughly smitten.

And as Kate gains strength, she knows that healing is never for itself alone. We are healed so that we may be part of others' healing. Kate yearns for the day when she, too, shall become part of the wall of protection and part of the lives of others. And she knows she will. First God heals us, and then he uses us in the great adventure that recovery is. If you've been part of the arm-in-arm march of recovery, you know its glory, power, and strength beyond any debate, opinion, or argument. We know what is true, and that truth can never be taken from us.

A THREE-STEP PRACTICE

Kate knows that all the help she will ever need is and always has been right in front of her. It's the same for us. Our job is to pay attention. It's to connect the dots so we know where the help is and how to access the music that never fails. One way to pay attention is a simple three-step practice for staying connected in our recovery that uses meaning, symbols, and meditation (see diagram):

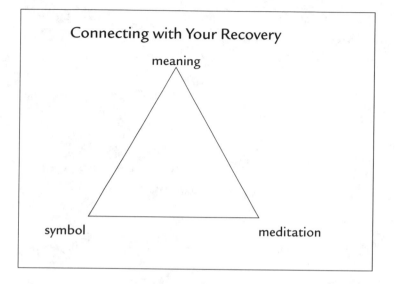

First, there is meaning. Meaning comes from experience, and experience is power. First we must reflect on our story, see and touch and feel again those moments when we experienced the "Power greater than ourselves." Look again at the faces and deeds of the great ones we have met along the way. Touch the bottomless meaning in the eyes of the children of recovering parents, where we have seen and thrill again at the realization of the hell they will miss because their parents were given and accepted the gift of recovery. Open up! Come alive! Recognize that recovery's fingerprints fill our book of days.

Second, there is symbol. We all need our symbols. Symbols are material things we invest with meaning. Symbols are material "packages" carrying a spiritual meaning that we can take anywhere and everywhere. They are "suitcases of the spiritual," if you will. Symbols are one way we as human beings communicate meaning. For example, a wedding ring is a symbol of marriage, the union of two people. Words, written or spoken, are symbols. Touch is a symbol. Smiles are symbols.

The importance and power of symbols is why the giving of chips or medallions is so helpful and important. But the symbol is only as powerful for us as the power we invest in it.

The origin of medallions goes back to the very beginning of the Twelve Step way of life and Sister Ignatia. An émigré from County Mayo, Ireland, Sister Ignatia founded what in effect was the first treatment center. She was a hospital nurse and friend of Dr. Bob's in Akron, Ohio. At that time, there was no medical help provided for the alcoholic. If there were to be hospital care, the person would have to be admitted under other presenting pathologies—that is, until fiery Sister Ignatia had enough of that!

At her insistence, a hospital in Akron opened a tiny six-bed ward for the primary treatment of alcoholism. She presented each person who entered her ward with a small plastic and cloth Sacred Heart badge. I don't know what she said when she handed her badges out, but the intent was clear. I imagine it went something like this: "Keep these badges on hand. The road is difficult, and we need all the help we can get. We need to keep our weapons at hand." The badges—carried, worn, or pinned to a shirt—were constant reminders, points of access to the power of recovery-love, always to be kept close and ready for instant use.

If we are not paying attention, it is easy to collect a drawer full of medallions as if they were bottle caps or meaningless trinkets. In her recovery history, Kate, for example, had collected many medallions. She had a drawer full of them. But her failure to access the meaning they carried rendered them powerless. Since she failed them, no medallion had sufficient power to carry her past the lies. As a result, she relapsed. None of these medallions carried the meaning of her wall of protection. But her newest medallion, which, incidentally, came from Dr. Bob's house itself, bristles with this new power. Kate keeps it close to her soul. Frequently, she will quietly, unobtrusively, reach into her purse and connect with the meaning and power of her medallion. Abundant strength is always at hand. It is now simply a matter of choosing to go there or not. Her defenders, who compose her wall of protection, always stand ready for battle. Once our symbol is "loaded," then what remains is to go there, use it, pull the trigger.

Third, there is meditation. As our Steps instruct, we "seek through prayer and meditation." Our Steps do not teach us to sit back and wait for something to happen. Faith must be sought. If we want it, we must go get it. If we want something, we must go where it is.

Meditation is a skill not easily acquired, especially if we have spent most of our lives choked with noise that hinders our ability to hear the Voice. Some people easily practice half-hour meditations. Good for them. For many of us, our best bet is the use of "mini-meditations." How long does it take to touch a medallion in our pocket and join our hearts and minds to whatever meaning we have packed into that symbol? How long does it take to call to mind an especially powerful moment in our recovery story? How long does it take to reach inside and connect with whoever stands in our wall of protectors? A million times I have practiced a mini-meditation by watching Jimmy R., whom we met all those pages ago, old and sick but going to his meeting in below-zero temps because, as he says, "Maybe there is someone there I can help."

Meditations come in all shapes and forms. What I am referring to here is meditation as "going where it is." Use your symbol. Work it. Go there. Meditation is staying connected to the meaning packed into our symbols. It is not possible to relapse or turn a deaf ear to where the Voice is calling us to go if we stay connected.

IT'S REWARD ENOUGH

There are those who would dismiss Kate's practice or our practice of meaning-symbol-meditation as sugar-coated fantasy. These people might call Kate's wall of protection and God speaking through her butterfly as "soft." They may say something like, "It's nice and all, but it is just too squishy for the real world."

These people have never sat in a roomful of miracles in the "real world." They have never looked at the salvaged faces among a group, seeing in them people who have lived endless excess. They haven't seen the mountain of a man who has wreaked havoc in many a bar but now abides in peace, looking and talking like the tender child that he truly is. And next to him is the woman who came back from the horrors of many attempted suicides. Next to them are other brothers and sisters who, though once firmly held in the mouth of the dragon, have come out free and flying.

If we have escaped the dragon's mouth, we know what is real and what isn't. The world has a thousand award ceremonies for those who excel at what the world values. So be it. But for those of us blessed to walk the recovery road, those of us who see with different eyes, having a right conscience and liking and honoring the person we see in our bathroom mirror every morning is reward enough. To be called to be part of a protective wall for another person is an honor beyond any acclaim or fame. Let others pursue whatever success they seek. But for us, what greater success exists in all the world than to stand with our peers, in service to God, witnessing the miracle of recovery blooming around us in such grand, glorious fashion?

SUCCESS THAT MATTERS

I'd like to end this chapter with an answer, if you will, or a reply to the man we referred to at the beginning of this chapter, the one who guessed he didn't need to be ashamed about being an alcoholic anymore. My response comes from a wise, grateful man in recovery who spoke to his brothers as they were just finishing treatment. His sentiments could be viewed as universal. I believe they are as true for any man, woman, or child in recovery from whatever addiction or connection with an addict there is. Here is what he said:

> Brothers, you are the best that ever was. You are the finest examples of what success is all about in this flawed, messy, often-absurd world of ours.
>
> Any ordinary man can play the world's game, win plaques and awards, and be celebrated as a success for these achievements. But success that matters comes not from collecting such pretty trifles, but from a life that turns the corner on honesty, looks deep into a troubled heart, and comes to grips with whatever problems are discovered there.
>
> Any ordinary man can make a lot of money and call that success. But it takes a real man to count his wealth in the number of true brothers he has covering his back and the willingness he has to go to any lengths to be there when a brother in need calls for help.
>
> Any ordinary man can win a fight when he outnumbers the enemy ten or twenty to one. But it is the man who fights on even when he feels alone and will not be stopped even when it appears he is fighting impossible odds that is the true success and more, the true hero.
>
> Any ordinary man can smile at the camera and live only for the strong light of fame. But those who count are those who go about their duty whether anyone else notices or not. These are souls minted in pure gold, who could care less for fame and consider a right, free conscience more than ample reward.

Any ordinary man can run his course if he has never been knocked down. The true success is the man who, though knocked down many times, has never failed to get up and try again. Only he knows the true meaning of glory; only he knows the battle-won sense of victory that comes from still standing tall after taking the enemy's best shot.

Any ordinary man can find security in his own strength or the thin, leaky protection of human power or position. It is the man who finds his strength in surrendering to God and walking with his brothers, head held high and bursting with pride, that is wealthier and more successful than any others who walk this earth.

Let others chase bobbles and trinkets. For us, it is to keep our eye on what counts and march toward that endless sunrise that alone satisfies. We become secure in the knowledge that our greatness comes from within. Nothing outside our band of brothers can take that greatness from us or is worth trading one ounce of what we share for anything that the world calls valuable.

Perception dictates truth. Let others value what they will. For us, we look within to our souls and feel the reflected glory of the souls of our brothers and the God who binds us together, and shout beyond any doubt or fear: Thank you, God, for allowing me fellowship with this band of men who are the best there ever was.

That's what he said, and that is what I believe as well. That is the truth. Beyond feeling shame, we have the right to feel soaring pride at who we are and what we are allowing God to fulfill in and through us.

QUESTIONS

1. Why does a successful program for you demand fellowship or community?
2. Who is part of your "circle of champions" or "wall of protection"?
3. Name a time when you needed fellowship. Then, name another time when you provided it to another.

MOVING ON TO CHAPTER 12

To be grateful for the program is also to take responsibility for carrying the message. Although that message is timeless, the way it is carried from generation to generation can change. We dare not confuse the content of the box for the box itself. The content is eternal. Boxes are not. True fidelity to a cause or mission is always creative fidelity. It is always about asking, "How can I best, in the here and now, be a servant to the message I hold so dear?"

CHAPTER 12

Loyalty to the Program: Creative Fidelity

Loyalty to the gift of the program is best accomplished by carry-ing the message the best we can in our own time in history. Times may change; the basics of the program do not. We best repay the debt we incurred by adapting the unchangeable basics of the program to our time in history. That is the "creative" part of creative fidelity. That is what justifies adding the concepts in this book to the "older, narrower" understanding of recovery.

I still remember the meeting. Somehow the smell of stale smoke and bad coffee seems as real now as it did then, even though it has been over twenty years ago. It was an open meet-ing. The guest speaker was a charismatic African American man from Dallas. In his deep, booming voice, he stated, "The Twelve Step program is God's greatest gift to the twentieth century." It made an impression on me. Since then, I've never experienced anything that would make me doubt his senti-ment. Twelve Step living works. The condition of the human heart has not changed. But the world has.

Someone living in the twentieth century experienced more change than anyone living in any other century in history. My generation could not imagine a world without cars. My children's generation could not conceive a world without television. My grandchildren can't imagine a world before computers, PalmPilots, and cell phones. Regardless of all the advances in science and technology, the nature of our species remains unchanged. What damages us as humans and what corrects that damage is the same today as it was yesterday. The Twelve Step program is a gift of spirit. It is about reaching into lives that could not be more lost, depleted, and savaged and making nothing short of miracles appear. I'm talking about bringing order out of total chaos. The gift is a recovery program that transforms despair into hope and places the feet of the totally, dismally lost onto the road leading back home. Twelve Step programs do this; they work.

The map of recovery that *Destination Joy* covers views addictions existing within the context of our humanity first and the path that naturally flows from that starting point. It is not meant to challenge or compare any other understanding of Twelve Step work. The overriding philosophy of this book has always been to encourage you, the reader, to look at your story—what does it tell you? Then, regarding what I have to say, take what you like and leave the rest.

TRADITION, BASICS, AND THE TWELVE STEP WAY OF LIFE

I am a traditionalist. I firmly believe in the basics of the Twelve Step program. My point here is not to diminish and certainly not to discredit a more traditional understanding of the scope of Twelve Step recovery. A cloud of doubt has always haunted me as I share the lessons I have learned on my journey of recovery. The doubt arose from these nagging questions: What right did I have to introduce anything new concerning our Twelve Step program? Who was I to say there were levels or stages of recovery? Who was I to place such emphasis on why we were called to find and follow the path to joy and abundance? Who was I to not only suggest we need to take seriously the phrase in the Fifth Step that deals with "the nature of our wrongs," but also to state that the meaning of that phrase can only be understood by "connecting the dots"? Who was I to say recovery is best understood by starting with the basic needs at the center of who we are as human beings? Who was I to suggest a model of recovery that demands granting the necessary room for and acceptance of whatever damage to the spirit there may be lurking on the Stage III Recovery level of our lives? Who was I to so plainly state that "recovery is always a love story" and give such primacy of place in recovery to "recovery-love"? Who was I to suggest anything? But how does a loyal devotee of anything show that fidelity other than by saying, "I can repay the gift of my recovery by sharing what I have learned along the way"?

GOING TO THE SOURCE—
THE JOURNEY BACK TO AKRON, OHIO

A former professor of mine used to say, "When in doubt, go to the source." So that is what I did a few years ago. I made the pilgrimage to Akron, Ohio, to talk with the spirits of our founders, which can still be powerfully felt at the places where the inspiration of the Twelve Step program was first given. I stood on the street in front of 825 Ardmore, Dr. Bob's house, where the first gatherings that eventually became Alcoholics Anonymous met. I sat on the couch in Dr. Bob's front room and at the kitchen table where Dr. Bob and Bill W. must have sat for countless hours listening to the birth of this great gift emerge from the grinding stones of their conversation. (The furniture pieces are replicas of the originals, but the space where it all happened is the same.) I stood on that holy ground and looked forward and backward down the decades to see millions of our brothers and sisters rise whole and new through the power of the program.

A Team to Be Proud Of

As I quietly sat in Dr. Bob's house, a scene of enormous affection flashed through my mind. Six of us "program people" were invited to do our thing at a college class dealing with substance abuse. The class was composed of forty or so people, mostly fresh-faced twenty-something kids with their whole lives before them. Some were taking the course as a requirement for obtaining degrees in other fields such as criminal justice, social work, or education. Some were in class because their parents were alcoholics or they feared a loved one "used too much." No doubt a few of the "loved ones" the students were concerned about were themselves.

What struck me, sitting in Dr. Bob's front room, was the incredible sense of continuity from Bob's time to our own. Because of what happened here in Dr. Bob's house, the six of us were speaking to that roomful of students. The times may have changed, but the basics of the message had not. The hearts of those in the fellowship from then to now had not changed. Loyalty to the basics was apparent and deeply touching. The team of us six grateful Twelve Steppers chose to speak to that college class years after Dr. Bob was gone.

First of those among us was Cap. He is one of those strong African American men who seem to be invincible. He is now the director of a day treatment program for court-ordered youth that society has thrown away. One moment in Cap's sharing seemed especially strong. As he talked about his kids, his face took on the kind of shocked, amazed look someone might have if they came upon a car wreck that left the street littered with blood and debris. His eyes looked up, but you could tell he was looking at something playing on the inside of his head. Cap said, "Some in my program are twelve- and thirteen-year-old kids who trust no one." Then the look of wonder went deeper as he said, "And fear no one because they have nothing left to lose." But there is Cap, in the trenches with the forces that would steal these lives before they ever began. Cap has been to the bottom, to prison, to Vietnam, around the world, and back here. Through him, his God grabs as many of these children as possible before they tumble away and are lost forever.

Then came Belle. She brims over with the gift of joy as she addresses the crowd of college kids. At various meetings we have attended, I've often thought, "She can hardly contain her joy and gratitude of the rewards of the promises given to her." But a different Belle addressed the class. She spoke of her alcoholic father. She told the class of her certainty that she would never drink like her father and hurt others the way he had. But it was that first drink during her early teen years that put her in a different place, a place she craved, a place of happiness and acceptance. Like Cap, Belle at times slipped into her thousand-yard stare where she was looking into the memories in her mind rather than the faces before her. She told of a time she was arrested for driving drunk and spent the night in jail. "That wasn't me," she said. "When I woke up and realized where I was, I was so ashamed of myself. That wasn't who I was."

As her drinking progressed, so did the situations she found herself in that "weren't her" either. Finally, she was given the gift of the First Step. Then came the slow, at times uneven, climbing out of the pit she was in while following her map of recovery. That was a long time ago, she said. Her mother recently presented her with her fifteen-year medallion. It was the same medallion her father had received at his fifteen-year celebration. Belle told the class that recovery is the greatest blessing that has come into her life, but it isn't free. Belle gets up every morning at five so she can do forty-five minutes of prayer and meditation before starting her day. It has become essential to her continued spiritual growth. "That first drink is only an arm's length away," she told the class. "And there is nothing in the world I won't do to make sure I never reach for it."

Pam addressed the crowd next. She has been a grateful, recovering member of Al-Anon for the past twenty-one years. Pam, like any affected person, blamed herself for her husband Dave's drinking. He drank because Pam was not smart enough, young enough, rich enough, or thin enough, she thought. It was only when she hit bottom and became ready to accept the help that always surrounded her that she found the program and started to grow. Pam told of the damage done to her two children during Dave's drinking career. Their sons were twelve and seven when Dave found recovery. Her oldest son, Paul, still lives with the scars. With tears in her eyes, she recounted how Paul was an exceptional soccer player ever since he was a little boy. Dave, of course, missed all his games in the early years. When he finally sobered up, he told Paul one afternoon he was coming to see him play soccer that evening. "Paul called his coach that same day and quit the team. He never played soccer again," she told the group. "He still has a hair trigger whenever there is even a hint of anything from his dad that sounds like loud, controlling behavior. And his dad has been sober for over twenty years," she told us.

Red-haired Casey was up next. She couldn't weigh a hundred pounds if she had bricks in her pocket, but she is a spiritual heavyweight. She started her sharing by clearly stating she had just five months' sobriety. She told of her nearly five-year stint in prison for killing a man while driving drunk. Like Belle, Casey also had a father who was an alcoholic, and Casey, too, vowed at an early age never to follow his lead. Among other tragedies in her life, she was raped in high school. No one seemed to care all that much. Her mother said she probably deserved it. Casey figured that if no one else cared about her, she must not be worth caring about. Alcohol (and every drug she could lay her hands on) took her, momentarily (the old lie powerfully at work), to a place where she did count and big people didn't hurt little people. Even after she was released from prison, Casey kept drinking and driving. She was picked up again and placed in the workhouse for another sixteen months. "God has to work harder for some of us than others," she said. As honest as a human being could be, she told the class she carried the man she killed—the husband and father she took away—in her heart and head every day. "I can't change the past; I can only take responsibility for the present moment now given me," she said. "And that is why I'm here talking with you" she said, "to keep the evil committee that lives in my head manageable."

The last one to speak to the group besides me was Willard, my dear companion in recovery for nearly twice the number of years most of the class had been alive. Like always, his words came right from his heart. After he sat down, I told the class what he never would about himself. I told them that a few years ago, I was having trouble finding a way to get to a prison in a different state to see the inmates I had been corresponding with for a long time. They wanted to see "the guy who wrote the books." What they were really asking, though, was, "Are we really important enough for him to visit us?" They wanted to know if they really mattered, or if all that "recovery-love" stuff I had been writing about was just another con.

At that time, Willard owned and flew a small Comanche airplane. No sooner had I mentioned the problem about how to make the visit happen when he said, "Let me know when you want to go. I'll fire up the Comanche and we'll get on up there." And like the true recovery warrior he is, he said, "We can't keep anyone waiting if they are reaching out their hands, you know."

That's what I wanted to tell the class about Willard and recovery. It's all about love. Nothing but recovery-love makes a difference.

Are there any other people anywhere we'd be more proud to walk with than those we meet in the fellowship? Where else can so many heroes of the spirit be found? We try to take what we have learned from having been found at the bottom, and we do all we can to bring light into this world. And such a beautiful light it is. Whether recovery is seen in a narrower or wider context, all there is, is love. Love is the primacy of recovery. Therefore, the road of recovery leads to love. That's what this book is all about.

I Asked Dr. Bob

Standing right there in Dr. Bob's front room, I was overwhelmed by the memory of that class. Situations just like our class, and literally countless other acts of love and service done by members of the fellowship, have graced human existence since 1935. I am constantly awed and inspired by the uncountable acts of heroism carried out by and in our fellowship. Who else lives closer to the flame of life? So, I asked Dr. Bob the best way I could if it was right to continue to press for this map of a wider understanding of recovery. I asked him if such thinking in any way dishonored or disrespected the program. The words came through a slight whiff of pipe smoke and with a voice that twinkled: "If it helps the fellowship, go for it." And so I did.

QUESTIONS

1. How do you feel you best express your loyalty to the program?
2. When was a time you acted out that loyalty?
3. What does the sentence "fidelity to the program is always creative fidelity" mean to you?

THE PROMISES OF THE BIG BOOK*

We are going to know a new freedom and a new happiness. We will not regret the past nor wish to shut the door on it. We will comprehend the word serenity and we will know peace. No matter how far down the scale we have gone, we will see how our experience can benefit others. That feeling of uselessness and self-pity will disappear. We will lose interest in selfish things and gain interest in our fellows. Self-seeking will slip away. Our whole attitude and outlook upon life will change. Fear of people and of economic insecurity will leave us. We will intuitively know how to handle situations which used to baffle us. We will suddenly realize that God is doing for us what we could not do for ourselves.

Are these extravagant promises? We think not. They are being fulfilled among us—sometimes quickly, sometimes slowly. They will always materialize if we work for them.

---

*From *Alcoholics Anonymous,* 4th ed., published by AA World Services, Inc., New York, N.Y., 83–84.

THE TWELVE STEPS OF
ALCOHOLICS ANONYMOUS*

1. We admitted we were powerless over alcohol—that our lives had become unmanageable.
2. Came to believe that a Power greater than ourselves could restore us to sanity.
3. Made a decision to turn our will and our lives over to the care of God *as we understood Him.*
4. Made a searching and fearless moral inventory of ourselves.
5. Admitted to God, to ourselves, and to another human being the exact nature of our wrongs.
6. Were entirely ready to have God remove all these defects of character.
7. Humbly asked Him to remove our shortcomings.
8. Made a list of all persons we had harmed, and became willing to make amends to them all.
9. Made direct amends to such people wherever possible, except when to do so would injure them or others.
10. Continued to take personal inventory and when we were wrong promptly admitted it.
11. Sought through prayer and meditation to improve our conscious contact with God *as we understood Him,* praying only for knowledge of His will for us and the power to carry that out.
12. Having had a spiritual awakening as the result of these steps, we tried to carry this message to alcoholics, and to practice these principles in all our affairs.

---

*From *Alcoholics Anonymous,* 4th ed., published by AA World Services, Inc., New York, N.Y., 59–60.

ABOUT THE AUTHOR

EARNIE LARSEN is one of Hazelden's top-selling authors. His book *Stage II Recovery: Life beyond Addiction* was published by Harper San Francisco in 1985 and is still in publication, having sold over 225,000 copies. His book *Stage II Relationships: Love beyond Addiction* was published by Harper San Francisco in 1987 and is also still in publication. These books explore the rebuilding of life after breaking a primary addiction. Larsen is well-known for coining the term *Stage II* in the recovery field. The term is now his official trademark.

A pioneer in the field of recovery, addiction, and unwanted behaviors, Larsen has written numerous motivational and self-help books along with producing audiotapes on a variety of topics ranging from managing interpersonal relationships to spirituality. He has also been referred to as an authority on issues such as codependency and addictive lifestyles.

As a lecturer, Larsen is known coast-to-coast and is sought after by industry and treatment centers. His seminars are frequently sold out, due in part to his unique simplicity and his "heart of America" folksy appeal. In addition, he has made appearances on radio and television throughout the world.

Larsen has written and created the Life Management Program, a cutting-edge program that shows people how to connect the dots of their recovery; he and his master trainers have been teaching this program for over twenty years in the United States and abroad. More information on this program can be found by calling 1-800-635-4780 or by going to his Web site at www.earnie.com.

Larsen's education includes an M.R.E. degree in theology and education from Loyola University Chicago and a master's degree in psychology from the Roman Catholic Redemptorist order for priests. He also has a degree in counseling with accreditation in chemical dependency and family counseling from the University of Minnesota.

A practicing counselor for thirty-five years, Larsen and his wife, Paula, live in Minneapolis, Minnesota. They have four grandchildren and one on the way, who Larsen says have taught him tons.

ABOUT HAZELDEN PUBLISHING

As part of the Hazelden Betty Ford Foundation, Hazelden Publishing offers both cutting-edge educational resources and inspirational books. Our print and digital works help guide individuals in treatment and recovery, as well as their loved ones.

Professionals who work to prevent and treat addiction also turn to Hazelden Publishing for evidence-based curricula, digital content solutions, and videos for use in schools, treatment and correctional programs, and community settings. We also offer training for implementation of our curricula.

Through published and digital works, Hazelden Publishing extends the reach of healing and hope to individuals, families, and communities affected by addiction and related issues.

For information about Hazelden publications,
please call **800-328-9000**
or visit us online at **hazelden.org/bookstore.**